MW01616166

"I was there at 'Iokane heiau day with my brothers and s it was an awesome experience to witness God's mana (spiritual power) revealed among his people."

**Kaho'okele Crabbe**
*Kumu Hula (Master Hula Instructor)*
*Hawaiian Language Kumu (Teacher)*

---

"Like the writer of the Apostolic Scriptures named Luke, I too can verify that what you are about to read is a true and accurate account of real events. But unlike Luke, it was not handed down to me for I was an eyewitness and active participant in the amazing events of March 14, 1998."

**Kahu (Pastor) Kealoha Kaopua**
*Calvary Community Church*
*Kailua-Kona, Hawai'i*

---

"I was one of the many people present at 'Iokane Heiau on March 14, 1998. From the testimony of many, Daniel has woven together a beautiful and accurate picture depicting the series of awesome events that happened that Saturday afternoon. I have never had an experience like that before or since."

**David M. Ross, Jr., PE**
*President*
*Ross Engineering, Inc.*

---

"It was a great privilege for me to be a part of the project that took place on March 14, 1998. I also witnessed the events that occurred at 'Iokane heiau that Saturday afternoon."

**Donna Jordan**
*Missionary for 31 years (12 years in Hawaii)*

# God of
# LIGHT

---

# God of
# DARKNESS

**Ke Akua o ke Ao, Ke Akua o ka Pō**
**The Chronicles of the Spiritual Battle for Hawai'i**

# Daniel Kikawa

**Published by:**
Aloha Ke Akua Ministries
P.O. Box 492325
Keaʻau, Hawaiʻi 96749
www.alohakeakua.org

Publisher's Cataloging-in-Publication Data
*(Provided by Cassidy Cataloguing Services, Inc.)*

Kikawa, Daniel.

    God of light, God of darkness : the chronicles of the spiritual battle
    for Hawaii / by Daniel Kikawa. -- 1st ed. -- Keaau, Hawaii : Aloha Ke
    Akua Pub., c2008.

        p. ; cm.

        ISBN: 978-0-9643595-1-2
        Includes bibliographical references.

        1. Hawaiians--Religion--History. 2. Christianity--Hawaii--History.
    3. Religious leaders--Hawaii--Biography. I. Title.

BL2630.H38 .K554 2008
299/.9242--dc22              0804

# Table of Contents

## Part Three — The 'Io Project

# Acknowledgments

This story is about one incident in the history of Ke Akua (God's) plan for Hawai'i. As important as it was, it was only one step in the staircase of many events ascending towards the fulfillment of God's plan. God's complete plan has not been fulfilled yet; we are still climbing!

This event could not have been possible without the many steps that came before it, upon which it was built. We must give credit to our kūpuna in Hawai'i, the brave adventurers who settled these islands; the priests of 'Io who strived to keep the knowledge of 'Io pure; Kamehameha, who unified these islands; 'Ōpūkaha'ia; Hewahewa, Lunalilo, Ka'ahumanu, Ke'ōpūolani who courageously overthrew the religion of Pā'ao before the missionaries arrived; the many missionaries who gave their lives here like Titus Coan, Hiram Bingham, Lorenzo Lyons; and the scores of Followers of Jesus who worked and prayed fervently for Hawai'i over the many years since then. We acknowledge many who faithfully did their part in the recent past like Henry Kahalehili, Ken Kekoa, Victor Borga, Mildred Brostek, Sam Sasser, David Shotwell and Roy Sapp.

We acknowledge others who have worked faithfully and continue to work in the assignments God has given to them. This is a Body of Christ effort! We acknowledge the faithfulness and work of James Marocco, Dan Chun, Wayne Cordeiro, Art and Kuna Sepulvida, Sam Webb, Ralph Moore, Danny

Lehmann, Bill Stonebraker, Cal and Joy Chinen, Francis and Caroline Oda, Alan Cardenas, Roy "Rocky" Sasaki, and many others. We want to make a special acknowledgement to the many that are not well known because their part in God's work here remains hidden. Your reward is truly great in Heaven for Ke Akua sees your humble faithfulness.

We are humbled to be a part of this awesome group of people that God has joined together in unity to fulfill His great plan for Hawai'i. We are humbled to be a link in the great progression of our ancestors stretching back into the misty past and streaming forward into God's bright and glorious future for our beloved islands. It is God and God alone who does it through His Spirit in us. To God alone be the Glory, Aloha Ke Akua (God is Love)!

## Special Acknowledgements

So many people were editors, advisors or helped me with this book that it is really a group effort. This fruit is also yours my 'ohana (family)!

Akea Eaton, Mom Eaton, Leon Siu, Kahu Kawika Kahiapo, Kaho'okele Crabbe, Aunty Malia Craver, Henry Williams, Ileili Tahauri, George Kaimiola, Kahu Hanalei Coleado, Kahu Kawewehi (Rusty) Pundyke, Eruera Kawe, Kahu Kealoha Kaopua, Island Breeze Hawai'i, Ann Kai-Millard and Peter Millard, Scott and Sandi Tompkins, Evans Elaban, Ken and Iris Tomita, Kahu John Truesdell, Jimmy Yamada, John and Joanne McCollum, Zennie Sawyer, Mariko Kikawa, Beatrice Kikawa, April Knudsen, Gail McConnell, Martha Morris, Robyn Kam, Richie Lambeth, David Ross, John Dawson, Don and Carol Richardson, Jacob Mau, and Herbert Hoefer.

Mahalo nui loa to the Aloha Ke Akua 'ohana, the 'Iokāne 'ohana and all of the people who were involved in the 'Io

Project, the island coordinators, mappers, intercessors and prayer warriors. So many of you were not mentioned in this book—Mahalo!

A special Mahalo to my wife Landa who has put up with me and has been my main confidant and advisor.

*In Memory of:*
Aunty Dolly Moke
Kahu Henry Kahalehili
Blend Apaka
Kahu Ken Kekoa
Robert Kikawa
Kahu Gaymond Apaka
Aunty Malia Craver
Mom Arlene Wainaha Ku`uleialoha Brede Eaton
Don Mapes

# Introduction

I have waited seven years to tell this story. It has taken that long to obtain permission from the matriarch of the 'Iokāne family; after all, much of this story is their family legacy, the 800-year-old prophecy and the promise of "The One" that was fulfilled on March 14, 1998. It has taken three more years to write it.

People who do not understand Hawaiian ways may wonder why I would need to ask permission and why the matriarch of the 'Iokāne family would not want their amazing story told. "*Why, they could be famous, and who wouldn't want such recognition?*" However, being famous and recognized is not a Hawaiian value; keeping family and spiritual integrity is. I needed to wait because to publish their story, even though I had a major part in it, would not be pono (right). The 'Iokāne family's matriarch waited until 'Io told her it was the pono time. It was well worth the wait. The blessings of God follow His right order. Once I received permission from the earthly authority to write this story, God told me it was time to share it with His people. I can now continue in the mission to which He called me many years ago: "***Tell all people that I (God) have this same story of faithfulness and love for them that I have for Hawai'i.***"

Therefore, in obedience to my Lord, I share this previously unrecorded chapter in the spiritual history of Hawai'i. It is a story of a voyaging people who followed God's leading to their promised land, of evil forces that nearly crushed them, and of a great time of redemption. It may seem like the stuff of legends, but I assure you it is true. And the most extraordinary part of this story is that God used ordinary people to carry out His plan. Yes, people who have faults, fail and fall into sin. It is a story of real Christians; and no, I am not talking about people who go to church. Going to church does not make one a Christian any more than sitting in a garage makes one a car. I mean people who have a living and real relationship with their God. When such people commit to obeying His will, anything is possible!

I am one of those ordinary people God used in His redemptive work in Hawai'i. It was my privilege to lead the 'Io Project in 1998, and to interview all the leaders mentioned in this story. Because of this, I could have told this story from a first-person perspective. But I have chosen to tell it in the third person, as an observer. It was easier for me to tell that way.

When I began writing, I struggled to know where to start this story. I decided it needed to be told from the beginning of the first settlers to Hawai'i. One cannot understand the fullness and majesty of God's omnipotent plan for these islands unless we start at the very beginning, at a time when the Hawaiian people launched boldly out in faith into the uncharted waters of the vast Pacific Ocean. At God's command, they set out in search of the home He had prepared for them, Hawai'i!

For this early era, information was sparse. This meant that, for this story to be told, the thin thread of the prophecy of "The One" and the sparse known Hawaiian history recorded in Part One of the book needed to be "filled in." Using historical and archeological data, oral histories, chants, interviews with kūpuna (Hawaiian elders) and their advice, and my knowledge of Hawaiian and Polynesian society and culture, the background environment for recorded incidents was created to reflect what, to the best of my knowledge, Hawai'i was like in those ancient days. Most of the names of characters in Part One are fictional or disguised, only the names of Pā'ao and Pili are not. However, because we have only a brief historical description of them, it was necessary to "fill in" their characters for the story. Therefore, part one is historical fiction based on the sparse knowledge of that ancient time and the prophecy of the "One." All other names of people or families are fictional or disguised and have no relationship to any real persons or families. Any names in Part One that are in common with any persons or families are entirely coincidental.

The incidents in the Interlude, Part Two and Part Three of the book are true to recorded history and to the best memory of those involved. Much of Part Three was taken directly from videotaped interviews or written reports of people involved in the 'Io Project that were recorded in March and April of 1998.

Some names of people, places and their locations throughout the book have been disguised in an attempt to keep curiosity seekers from private, family sacred sites. The names disguised include the names of Moke, the 'Iokāne family, and their family heiau (temple). Unless a heiau was in a well known public location, I did not mention its name to prevent curiosity seekers from intruding on private land or tromping on precious archeological sites.

If anyone would not believe my story because they cannot trace certain names and people, that is their kuleana (their business). Being believed is not as important to me as protecting the people in this book, the people of Hawai'i, and the land. Let readers decide for themselves whether the things written in this book are true or not!

My hope and prayer is that this book will encourage people everywhere who have been ashamed of their cultural identity to realize the great love of God for them and the culture that flows from who He created them to be.

Aloha Ke Akua!

(God is Love)

*Daniel Kikawa*

# Glossary

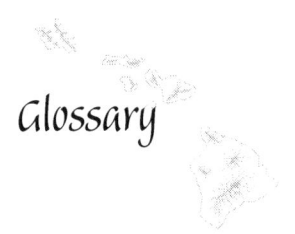

Ahupuaʻa—pie-shaped Hawaiian land division extending from the mountains to the sea

ʻĀina—the sky, ocean, land and all of the flora and fauna in them

Akua—god

Akualele- spiritual fireball or meteor usually sent by kahuna ʻanāʻanā (black witchcraft priests) to destroy people

Aliʻi—royalty, chief or chiefess

Aliʻi nui—high chief

Aloha—love, affection, compassion, mercy, sympathy, kindness, grace, charity

ʻAwa or kawa—drink used in ceremonies throughout Polynesia

Ehu—reddish-brown hair color of some strains of Polynesians

Hale—house

Hānai—unofficial adoption or fostering of a child

Haole—Westerner, white person

Heiau—ancient Hawaiian place of worship

Imu—underground oven

ʻIo—the One Creator God, also endemic Hawaiian hawk which is his symbol

Kahu—pastor or guardian

Kāhuli—rare indigenous land snail

Kahuna ʻanāʻanā—practitioner of sorcery, black magic

Kahuna Nui—high priest

Kahuna—priest, expert in any profession

Kalo—Hawaiian for *taro*, the starchy root made into poi, a staple food in Polynesia

Kamaʻāina—native-born person

Kaona—hidden meanings, plays on words

Kapu—forbidden, sacred, taboo

Kāula—prophet, seer

Koa—fearless, brave, also a warrior or soldier

Kukui—candlenut tree with oily nuts used for lighting, medicine and adornment

Kumu hula—master hula instructor

Kumulipo—Hawaiian creation chant

Kūpuna—grandparent, ancestor, anyone in grandparent's generation

Loʻi—irrigated terrace for growing taro

Lōkahi—unity, harmony, peace

Luakini—temple at which human sacrifices were offered

Makaʻāinana—Hawaiian commoner

Malihini—guest, visitor, stranger, newcomer

Malo—male loincloth

Mana—supernatural or divine power, authority

Manaʻo—thinking or knowledge that comes from the naʻau (stomach) not the poʻo (head)

Maori—native people of Aotearoa (New Zealand)

Marae—Polynesian temple or meeting house

Mū—official executioners and procurers of sacrifice victims

Naʻau—intestines, heart, soul, innermost being

ʻOhana—extended family, kin group, large family unit

ʻŌhiʻa—indigenous hardwood tree

ʻOki—to cut, sever, separate

Pono—rightness, good, excellence, proper

Puʻu—hill, mound or peak

Pua—flower, child

Tūtū—grandparent

Tūtū Wahine—grandmother

Tūtū Kāne—grandfather

# People and Places

Akea Eaton—Daniel's hānai (adopted) brother from Maui

Alan Cravalho—pastor from Honokaʻa, Big Island, who went to Waimanu Valley

Aloha Ke Akua—ministry founded by Daniel Kikawa, Kawika Kahiapo, Leon Siu

Ben and Lydia—Leaders of Kehilat O Ka Mesia, a Messianic/Hawaiian congregation on Kauaʻi

Beth Naholowaʻa Murph—Key ʻIo Project leader and intercessor from the Big Island

Big Island—the island of Hawaiʻi

Daniel Kikawa—pastor, author, founder of Aloha ke Akua ministry

Dean Spencer—pastor from Papakōlea, Oʻahu

Delbert—hunter who led pastor Alan and George into Waimanu Valley

Delfin Cravalho—Pastor Alan Cravalho's wife

Gaymond Apaka—pastor of New Hope church in Hilo

George Kaimiola—Key ʻIo Project leader on Maui

George Ruiz—worship leader who went with Pastor Alan to Waimanu Valley

Henry ʻŌpūkahaʻia—young Hawaiian man who converted to Christianity in New England, whose memoirs resulted in first missionaries to Hawaiʻi

Hewahewa—high priest at time of Kamehameha's death, descendant of Pāʻao

ʻIo—Creator God of Polynesia

Iokepa and Kepola—elders of Kehilat O Ka Mesia, a
Messianic/Hawaiian congregation on Kaua'i
Island Breeze—a Polynesian Christian ministry in Kailua-
Kona, also performs the lū'au show at the King
Kamehameha Hotel
Jacob Mau—Key 'Io Project leader on Maui
John Kūpuna—pastor, leader of the Halawa Valley team on
Moloka'i
John Truesdell—pastor from Hilo, descendant of Pā'ao
Kahiki—Hawaiian for Tahiti or a foreign place
Kahu Mau—pastor from Hana, Maui
Kalākaua—last king of Hawai'i
Kanaloa (Ta'aroa)—to some Hawaiians he is the personifica-
tion of evil
Kāne—One of the ancient Hawaiian trinity, creator of man,
aka Atea in Marquesas, also the name of man who is
made in his image
Kaulana Correa—Maui 'Io Project coordinator
Kawika Kahiapo—pastor, founder of Aloha Ke Akua
Kealakekua—large bay on the Big Island where Capt. Cook
arrived, was killed; also where Henry Opukaha'ia left
for New England
Keaukaha—Hawaiian homestead in Hilo
Kehilat O Ka Mesia—Messianic/Hawaiian congregation on
Kaua'i
Kepola and Iokepa—elders of Kehilat O Ka Mesia, a
Messianic/Hawaiian congregation on Kaua'i
Kohala—northwestern district of the Big Island
Kū—one of the ancient Hawaiian trinity who was trans-
formed into the god of war by Pā'ao
Landa Kikawa—Daniel's wife
Leon Siu—founder of Aloha Ke Akua
Lono—one of the ancient Hawaiian trinity, god of peace
Moke—descendant of 'Iokāne family, "The One"

Nalani Subiono—North Big Island 'Io Project coordinator

'Ōpūkaha'ia—young Hawaiian man who converted to Christianity in New England, whose memoirs resulted in first missionaries to Hawai'i

'Oro—bloodthirsty Tahitian god of war, the Hawaiian god Kū took on his characteristics after Pā'ao

Pā'ao—High priest, navigator, warrior, sorcerer from Tahiti, arrived circa 1200 AD, said to have brought human sacrifice to Hawai'i

Pali—Moke's wife

Paoakalani—*kumu hula* (hula master) of Island Breeze and Kamehameha descendant

Pele—goddess of volcanoes, was unknown in Hawai'i until after Pā'ao came

Pō—night, darkness, chaos or hell, realm of gods

Ra'iatea—one of the main islands of Tahiti (Society Islands) and seat of religion of Ta'aroa/'Oro

Ta'aroa—false creator god of Polynesia

Tammy Ruiz—wife of George who went with Pastor Alan to Waimanu Valley

Taputaputea—main temple of the religion of Ta'aroa/'Oro, located on Ra'iatea

Tex—Pastor James Texeira, pastor of Solid Rock Ministries in Kona, key 'Io Project leader

Tim Murph—Husband of Beth Naholowa'a Murph and key 'Io Project leader on the Big Island

Ty—wife of Delbert who led Pastor Alan and George into Waimanu Valley

Waha'ula—1st temple of human sacrifice built by Pā'ao on the Big Island

Waimanu Valley—remote valley in Honoka'a, Big Island

Waipi'o Valley—sacred valley in Honoka'a, Big Island before Waimanu Valley

# Maps

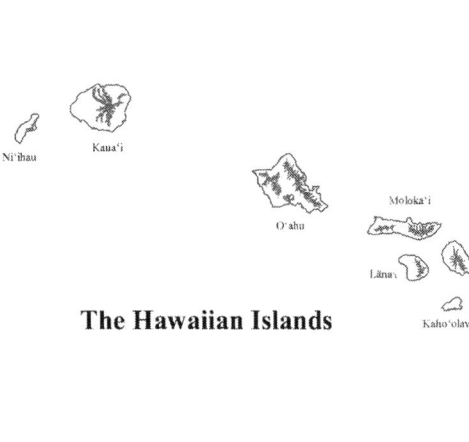

## The Hawaiian Islands

Niʻihau

Kauaʻi

Oʻahu

Molokaʻi

Lānaʻi

Kahoʻolawe

Maui

Hawaiʻi
(Big Island)

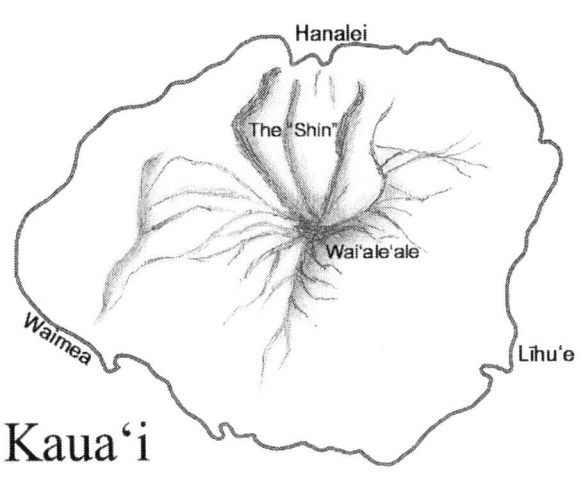

## Kauaʻi

Hanalei

The "Shin"

Waiʻaleʻale

Waimea

Līhuʻe

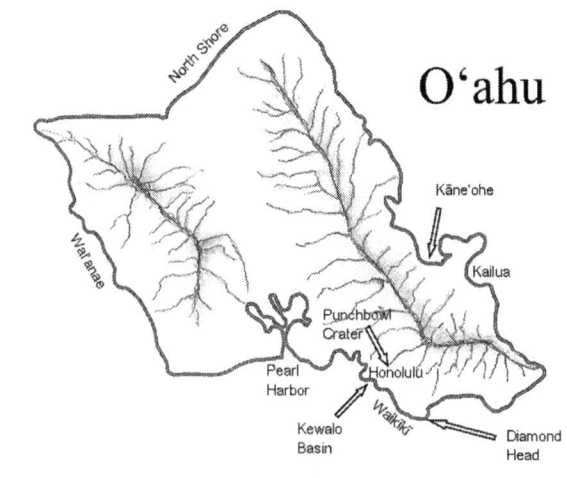

O'ahu

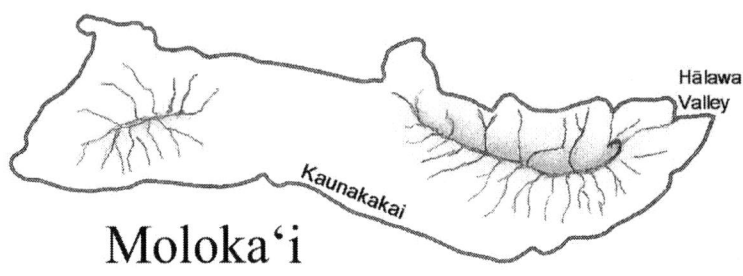

Moloka'i

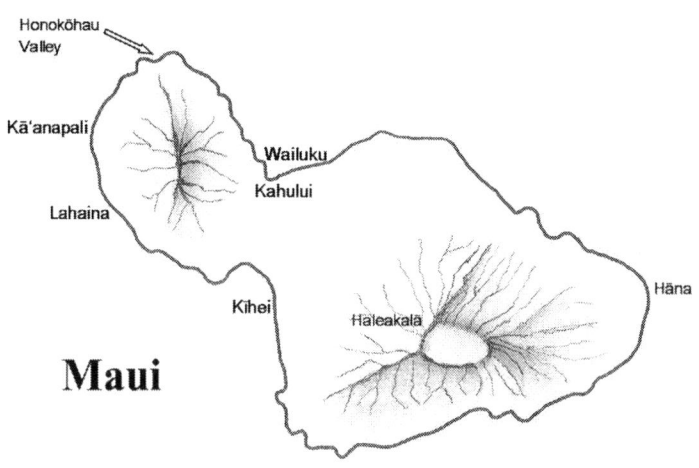

Maui

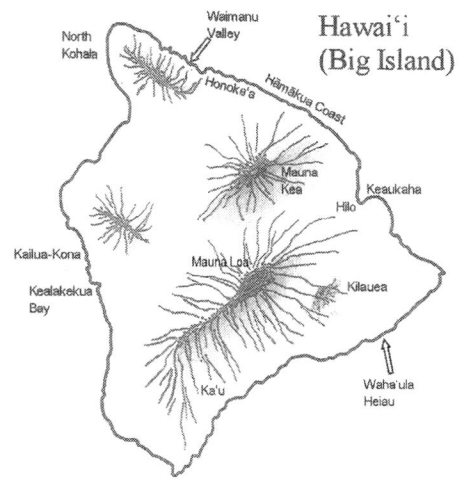

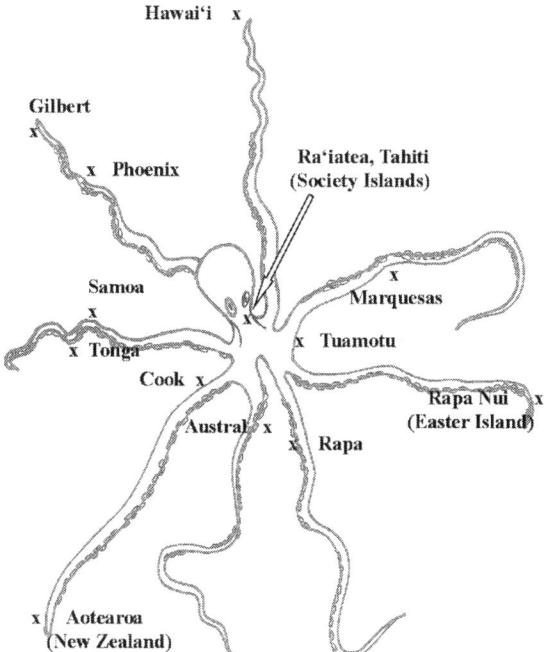

# Polynesia
In The Grip of Ta'aroa

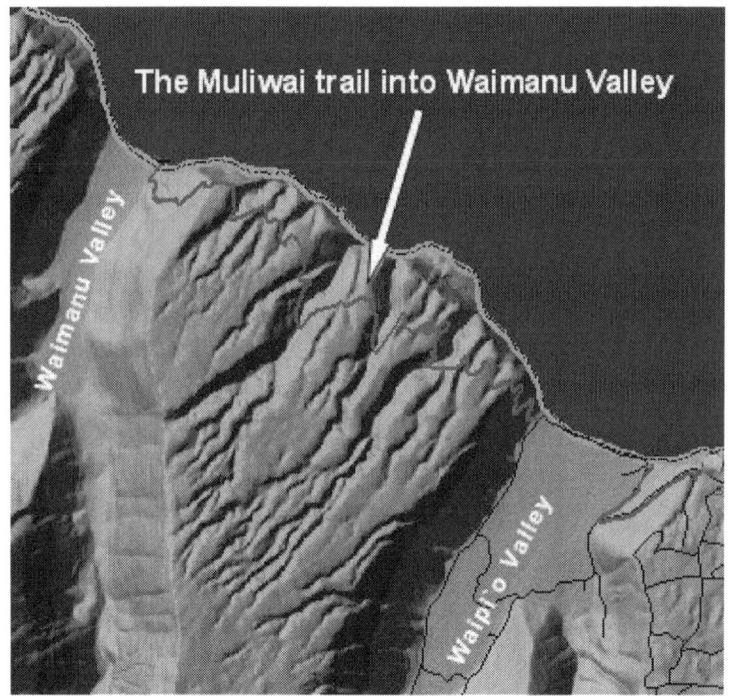

The Muliwai Trail connecting Waipi'o Valley and Waimanu Valley
Hawai'i (Big Island)

# Photos

Hōkūleʻa Voyaging Canoe

Hōkūleʻa in Tahiti

Taputapuatea Marae (temple), Ra'iatea, Society Islands (Tahiti)
The main temple of 'Oro, Tahitian god of war, it is said to have had the most human sacrifice in all of Polynesia.

Taputapuatea Marae (temple), Ra'iatea, Society Islands (Tahiti)

Human Sacrifice at Otahieite (Tahiti) with Capt. Cook
John Webber 1777

The restored Pu'ukoholā heiau dedicated to Kūkā'ilimoku, Hawaiian War God

Hawaiian Heiau (temples) shortly before the overthrow of the Kapu System

Execution of a kapu breaker
Jacques Etienne Victoire Arago, 1819

Execution of a kapu breaker
Jacques Etienne Victoire Arago, 1819

Henry ʻŌpūkahaʻia

Henry ʻŌpūkahaʻia Gravesite with Kealakekua Bay in the Background

Warrior chief of Kamehameha
with Western Sword
Jacques Etienne Victoire Arago, 1819

Kamehameha, 1816

Liholiho, Kamehameha II

Liliuʻokalani, Last Monarch of Hawaiʻi

Bible Box

Missionary Preaching

Waimanu Valley

Switchback trail up the 1200 foot Waipi'o Valley wall. The mouth of Waimanu Valley bay can be seen in the distance.

Waimanu Valley

The Historic Kailua Bay with the replica of Ahuʻena heiau in the foreground on the shore of Kamakahonu Bay. Across Kamakahonu Bay can be seen the Kailua pier, under which lies the Plymouth Rock of Kona and behind that, the first Christian Church in Hawaiʻi, Mokuʻaikaua.

Island of Kauaʻi
Mount Waiʻaleʻale in the background with its summit, as usual, shrouded in clouds.

Praying over sacrificial stone

Heiau entrance, doorway of trees, Kaua'i

Asking permission to enter heiau from the kahu (caretaker) of the heiau

Praying on a Heiau

Well at heiau used for washing sacrificial victims

Praying before entering heiau

Miles of barren lava fields below the active Kīlauea Crater

Lava Ledge

Dead tree Landa saw in her vision
above Halawa Valley

Bubble helicopter picking up Daniel, Landa and Zennie on the mountains above
Halawa Valley

One side of the clouds rolling back like a scroll
at 'Iokāne

Moke praying – notice the line of clouds still rolling back

# Part One
# Ancient Hawai‘i

# 1
# The Long Voyage

*"From one ancestor He made all nations to inhabit the whole earth, and He allotted the times of their existence and the boundaries of the places where they would live, [27]so that they would search for God and perhaps grope for Him and find Him—though indeed He is not far from each one of us. [28]For 'In Him we live and move and have our being'; as even some of your own poets have said, 'For we too are His offspring.'"*

—Acts 17:26-28 NRSV

Many centuries ago, the Polynesians set sail at the command of their God, the ancient chants of 'Io commanding them ever eastward toward the rising sun, to their final destination, the place He had lovingly prepared for them, to Hawai'i!

———

There! Barely visible against the angry, blackened skies rose a speck of frightened humanity. Like a tiny cork bobbing wildly, it appeared for an instant and then disappeared, sucked into the deep trough of another mountainous wave rising out of the treacherous sea.

Above the pounding waves and howling winds one could hear the cries of children as their mothers and elders struggled to calm their fears. Mingled with these cries could be heard the sounds of squealing pigs and whimpering dogs. Flashes of lightning revealed women, children and beasts beneath a canopy of woven grass, tree bark, and sticks, huddled together desperately against the slashing rains. This fragile canopy was lashed upon a platform joining two wooden hulls: a voyaging canoe of the Polynesians. Although the twin hulls were over forty feet each, they seemed but toothpicks, twisting and groaning in the massive swells, straining against lashings made of fibrous plants. Like a man bound and fighting against his binding, the hulls seemed to strain and twist to break free and scatter the tiny canoe and its cargo like so many twigs.

Upon these hulls, a bronze-skinned and powerfully built people could be seen holding steady in the powerful swells and currents. Fervent prayers and chants gave hope on these endless days. If one dared draw close, one could hear the priest chanting words of faith, the sacred command of 'Io, "*Move on, O Whakatau, move on to Hawaiki, establish there thy house, as though it were under the sacred care of 'Io.*" 'Io, the sacred name of the creator of all things.[1]

Though tossed amidst the sometimes merciless Pacific Ocean, these ancient mariners navigated by way of the wind, waves, stars and birds—wayfinding, they called it.[2] It was an understanding of nature deeply ingrained in these people. It was the mysteries of 'Io making wise their trusting hearts. They were following the ancient prophecy of the Star of Gladness which they called Hōkūle'a. They knew that after the storms relented, 'Io would bend a rainbow in the heavens and use rays of light as arrows to break forth in the light of dawn, the promised island in the midst of the sea.[3]

In times of calm waters and quiet nights, they gazed deeply into the starlit skies and were awed by the presence of the Almighty. His beacons of light would guide their ocean paths and His breath would fill their sails as their hulls gracefully skimmed the liquid space beneath.

Hungry and weather-beaten, but full of faith, they journeyed on until at last, on the far horizon, the Hawaiian Islands were birthed from the sea! It was an expression of 'Io's love waiting patiently to welcome these weary seafarers of old. Mighty 'Io the Creator of All Things, 'Io the Eternal, who ever was, is now, and ever shall be. They built their home there in that untouched paradise, under the sacred care of 'Io. It was a paradise hard for modern minds to imagine: no mosquitoes, flies, rats, scorpions, centipedes, snakes, fleas, or other pesky and irritating vermin of today. None of these could survive the great expanse of ocean on their own; they only could be brought by man.

Among these first brave voyagers to Hawai'i was the 'Iokane family. In obedience to 'Io, they built their family heiau,[4] as the Hawaiians called their temples of worship, in obedience to 'Io on the northwest finger of the island of Hawai'i, a place known today as North Kohala.

The family heiau was a place of peace, unity, joy, and aloha (unconditional love). It was a sanctuary where families would gather to learn of their God from the kahuna nui, the high priest. There were areas in the heiau for circumcision and for a cleansing ritual similar to baptism. It was a place for marriages, baby dedications, and funerals. It was the family meeting site where all were welcome and yet, it was a place of great holiness and reverence.

Here the 'Iokāne family worshipped their God in peace for 700–800 years...until the Great Sorcerer came!

# 2
# The Kāula

*"The names by which the Supreme Being is called are various and expressive. Almost everywhere they are uttered only with reverence…The most widely distributed names fall into three groups, denoting respectively fatherhood, creative power and residence in the sky. The name 'father' is applied to the Supreme Being in every single area of the primitive culture when he is addressed or appealed to…Among the Koryaks he is 'The One Above' or 'The Master Above,' while his Ainu name is 'The Divine Sky-Lord'… Among the Yoshua Indians of the American North-West he has a beautiful name, 'The Giver'.…As regards morality, the primitive Supreme Being is without exception unalterably righteous.…"*

—Wilhelm Schmidt, *The Origin and Growth of Religion*

Kalanikoa ʻIokāne was known by his people simply as "The Kāula," the Hawaiian word for prophet. The ʻIokāne family was one of the most influential and powerful families in Hawaiʻi. Their heiau (temple)—one of the oldest and most important in Hawaiʻi—was built for ʻIo, the supreme God: ʻIo the Creator, ʻIo the Water of Life, ʻIo the God of Aloha (unconditional love), ʻIo the All Powerful. There were many titles for his God, all speaking about his infinite power, wisdom and aloha.

In the morning, the Kāula could usually be found sitting cross-legged on a flat rock high above the family heiau. From his perch, he could admire the lush green Kohala Mountains rising to meet the clouds behind him. And because North Kohala juts out like a finger from the greater mass of the Big Island,[1] he also had a panoramic view of the Pacific Ocean on three sides. Across those sparkling blue waters, he could see Haleakalā, the island of Maui's huge volcano, floating above the distant clouds.

Most days, the Kāula felt complete peace in this beautiful setting, but not today. During his prayers at sunrise, 'Io had spoken to him clearly. Mostly, 'Io spoke to him as a knowing feeling, deep in his "na'au," his innermost being.[2] But today he heard 'Io speak as clear as a mountain stream. 'Io had asked him to do something that made him shiver. How could he do this painful thing 'Io had asked of him? And yet, he always obeyed. 'Io had proven himself over and over to the Kāula that he was a God who loved his people. The Kāula could not understand many of the things 'Io had told him to do in the past, but he had done them in faith. 'Io's wisdom always proved pono.

"*Pono, ah, the depth and beauty of the word!*"[3] the Kāula thought. He recalled what his tūtū kāne (grandfather) taught him as a young boy.

Tūtū kāne had told him, "*Kalanikoa, pono is 'rightness,' you are pono when you are right with your creator, right with men, and right with the 'āina.*"

"*Tūtū, what is the 'āina?*" he had asked. He already knew the answer but he loved to hear tūtū say it.

"*Ku'u lei (my dear one), the 'āina encompasses the land, sea, sky and all of the animals and plants that live in them. When all you do is pono with 'Io, your fellow man and the 'āina, you will have lōkahi.*"

"*What is lōkahi?*" Kalanikoa asked innocently.

"*Lōkahi means in perfect harmony, unity and peace. Things are lōkahi when you are pono with 'Io, the people and the 'āina. We call this perfect balance the lōkahi triangle. When it is out of balance, you will need ha'aha'a (humility) to see why it is out of balance and how to make it right. And, Kalanikoa, do you know what holds the lōkahi triangle together?*"

"*Aloha, tūtū! Without aloha, nothing else will work!*"

"*Good!*" said tūtū kāne as he lifted Kalanikoa onto his knee. "*Aloha sustains everything! 'Alo' means 'in the presence of' and 'ha' means 'the divine Spirit,' the breath of 'Io. It is the Spirit of 'Io that sustains all things.*"

Kalanikoa stared thoughtfully into tūtū's eyes. "*So that's why we greet people with aloha and bless them with aloha when they leave?*"

"*Yes, ku'u lei. And remember, you cannot aloha some and hate others, that is not possible. If you aloha, you aloha everyone. You can hate the evil that people do but you must always aloha them. Never forget these things, Kalanikoa, because only when the triangle is in balance can a person or society be at perfect peace!*"

The Kāula smiled at the warm memory of his beloved tūtū kāne. If only he could find such peace today. The words of 'Io that morning had disturbed his lōkahi triangle, and the Kāula struggled to regain balance. On this, of all days, he needed to be in the lōkahi triangle. He needed to see clearly for he could feel a growing disturbance in the 'āina.

One sign came from the wind. The Kohala area is famous for its blustery 'Āpa'apa'a[4] winds, but this day the earth and sea were still, like a child holding its breath, suspended, waiting. The Kāula sensed the 'āina knew something fearful was coming. The air felt heavy and foreboding. From his lofty perch, the Kāula gazed over the 'āina to see if he could discover the source of the disturbance. Out over the channel between the Big Island and Maui stood rows of long white clouds, like waves frozen overhead. Far below, he could see his family heiau, built by his ancestors when they arrived here a thousand years before. He recalled the stories tūtū kāne told him, and ancient chants about his people's long voyage to this place. A voyage led by their God, 'Io—'Io, the Sacred, 'Io the Beloved Father of All Men, 'Io, the God of Compassion and Mercy, 'Io the Creator of All Things.

The Kāula had been taught the ways of 'Io by tūtū kāne, who chose Kalanikoa as a boy to be the Kahuna Nui of the family heiau. He had often asked his grandfather, *"Why did you pick me?"* Tūtū kāne would just smile and say, *"You will find out why; 'Io told me you were 'The One'.* He would never tell him more. But before tūtū kāne died, he reminded Kalanikoa once more, *"Remember, a time of great trials will come upon our people that will last for many generations. Listen to 'Io, he will speak in a still and quiet voice in your na'au (innermost being). He will tell you what to do. The future of our people will depend on you. Your decisions will cause pain and suffering for the present generation, but make your decisions not for the present, but for the 'pua' (flowers / children) of the generations to come."*

The Kāula knew this time of great trials was near because of the near total corruption of the worship of 'Io in Hawai'i.[5] 'Io's ways were simple and pure, open to anyone who desired to know him. However, to gain prestige and power over their people, other priests of 'Io had created long chants and rituals they deemed necessary to gain the favor of and to receive communication from 'Io. The Kāula saw through their schemes. *"Of course only they knew the right chants and rituals so all their people had to come to them."* They said his name was too sacred for the maka'āinana (the common people) and that only the priests were holy enough to use his name. The Kāula knew his God loved all his children equally and without distinction. 'Io was always near to all of his children and any of them could call upon him. Some of these priests wielded power to create signs and wonders, but this power did not come from 'Io! And now many spoke of a powerful sorcerer named Pā'ao!

The Kāula sighed and rubbed his aching bones. Already the disturbance in the Lōkahi Triangle was taking its toll on his aged body. The Kāula had trained for over 40 years before he had been deemed ready to become the kahuna nui of the 'Iokāne heiau. He had served as high priest for many years since then. It seemed ages since he was a wide-eyed boy, hearing the chants of the great journey for the first time. He recalled one of the first chants he learned, the one about the creation of the universe, *"Io dwelt within the breathing space of immensity. The universe was in darkness, with water everywhere. There was no glimmer of dawn, no clearness, no light. And He began by saying these words, that He might cease being inactive, 'Darkness become a light-possessing darkness.' And at once light appeared."*[6]

He had learned that at the dawn of creation all was an eternal void, emptiness and blackness that cannot be fathomed by fragile human minds. Then, 'Io spoke and light streamed forth from the corridors of eternity. The land, sea and sky appeared. The moon and stars were set to shine in darkness. Soon, nature's song could be heard filling all the earth. Yet, the land, the 'āina, was not complete. Neither creature nor beauty could satisfy the longing of him who spoke all things into existence. Thus was Kumuhonua, the first man, fashioned from the red clay in the image of his Creator, and Keolakūhonua, the first woman, formed from his rib.[7] Creator and creation communed peacefully in the soft brilliance of the 'āina in that sacred first land. Kumuhonua and

Keolakūhonua had much aloha for their Akua (God), Most High...until the great fall. The woman was enticed by the great Moʻopeloa, the lizard/serpent of lies and flattery,[8] to disobey her God, and the man followed.

Many years later, after evil increased and filled the whole earth, ʻIo had called upon his servant, Nuʻu, the ancestor of all men, to build a large canoe with a house on top of it. ʻIo told Nuʻu he would flood the earth to cleanse it of sin. When the great flood came, Nuʻu took his wife, their three sons and their wives, and many animals on board the huge canoe. The rains lasted many days and nights and the waters remained for many days after that. When Nuʻu finally landed on dry land, ʻIo gave him a sign, the ānuenue or rainbow. This is why the rainbow is a symbol of ʻIo.[9] All Polynesians, like the Kāula, could chant their genealogies back to Nuʻu, the great ancestor of all men.

These musings of the Kāula were shattered by a familiar trumpeting sound. Conch shells! These shells were used by the Hawaiians to announce an arrival, to call people to meetings and to sound an alarm!

The Kāula listened again, holding his breath, hoping it was not so, it was an alarm! Conches were blowing far to the north. The Kāula rose to his feet, involuntarily shivering as a chill crept up his spine. He whispered to the ʻāina around him, "So...Pāʻao comes!"

# 3

# The Sorcerer Comes

*"Beware of Te Ma, 'The Unclean One.' He is always near!"*
— Chant from the Tainui Maori House
of Sacred Learning

*O*ut of breath and covered with a sheen of sweat, the bronze-skinned runner knelt at the Kāula's feet and panted out his urgent message. *"Pā'ao comes! Pā'ao the great sorcerer, he comes!"* The messenger's face was etched with terror. *"Pā'ao's fleet of war canoes approached so swiftly and silently, we did not have time to gather the men from the mountains or from the sea. Kāula, what should we do? He...is upon us!"*

The Kāula spun around and looked again at the ocean to the north. How could it be! In those few moments a massive fleet of war canoes had appeared out of nowhere! *"A powerful sorcerer he is!"* exclaimed the Kāula. The war canoes had already overtaken several fishing canoes that were fleeing toward the shore. Even from that great height he could see spears flying, bodies in the water and the dark red stains spreading around them. Some war canoes were already landing! The Kāula immediately remembered the words of ʻIo to him that morning. The timing to do what ʻIo asked of him was suddenly crystal clear. It was now!

There was no way they could win. No way could they defeat this massive, disciplined army. There was no way they could even gather the women and children in time to flee. To avoid further bloodshed and save his people, he must do as ʻIo had told him. He must meet Pāʻao immediately and step down as high priest of his heiau and leader of his people. He must do the most difficult thing he had ever done in his life. He must turn his sacred family heiau and his people over to Pāʻao. He must do this because it was the only way that the second part of the prophecy, "The Promise," would be fulfilled. He remembered what ʻIo had told him that morning, *"Kāula, you must step down from your post as high priest and turn your heiau over to the one who does not worship me. If you do this, someday, many generations from now, one of your descendants will restore this heiau to the worship of me."*

Before any more blood was shed, he must meet Pāʻao and concede his position to him. The Kāula rushed down the hill, but it seemed to be just a dream. How could his world be so suddenly shattered? How did this all begin![1]

Many Tahitians had migrated to Hawaiʻi in the years since the ʻIokāne family first arrived. They and other Polynesian voyagers had been welcomed with aloha and integrated peacefully with the Hawaiian people. Some had left Tahiti to escape the tyranny of the family of Pāʻao. The Kāula had heard stories from these refugees of Tahiti's constant warfare, harsh kapu (taboos) and awful human sacrifices. Some of these Tahitians were worshippers of 'Io also and came to find a safe haven where they could worship him in peace.

These Tahitians told the Kāula that the chiefs of Vavau (Bora Bora), had conquered the island of Ra'iatea, the sacred center of religion in Tahiti. Although the Vavau chiefs knew of 'Io,[2] they established an oppressive religious system on Ra'iatea at the temple called Taputapuatea. Here they worshiped 'Oro, the bloodthirsty god of war. 'Oro demanded more human sacrifice than any other god in Polynesia. He was the son of Ta'aroa, the false creator god who replaced 'Io in Tahiti and in most of central Polynesia. Followers of Ta'aroa, a god who often took the form of a giant squid or octopus, believed Polynesia belonged to Ta'aroa. His head lay at Taputapuatea in Ra'iatea, the center of Polynesia, and his tentacles stretched out to hold firmly in its grip all of the Polynesian triangle.[3] Unlike 'Io, to whom man was sacred and not to be killed, Ta'aroa and his son, 'Oro demanded the blood of humans. The Kāula could not comprehend the horrors described by the Tahitian refugees. They told of voyaging canoes with sacrifices lined up on their decks in sequence; a turtle, a man, an *ulua* (Jackfish), a man, a shark, a man. They spoke of men being used as rollers to haul these heavy double-hulled voyaging canoes up on shore. They described how the human sacrifices were drilled through the head and then strung from the trees with ropes, and how human heads filled the walls of Taputapuatea. The Kāula could see in his mind's eye, this menacing and gruesome place, with rotting bodies hanging from the trees and the human skulls leering from its walls.

Pā'ao's family joined forces with the chiefly line from Ra'iatea. Together, these chiefly families rallied great numbers of warriors and formed a large fleet of war canoes built for speed and silence. They also had designed paddles and paddling techniques for speed and silence.[4]

With these techniques and their special canoes, they surprised and conquered the other islands of western Tahiti. They were given the name *Porapora i te hoe mamu* (first born of the silent paddle) and *Porapora i te nuu ta rua* (first born of the fleet that strikes both ways).[5]

The Kāula had heard of Pāʻao before. He was told of an unusually charismatic man who came from Tahiti for a visit. He had light skin and ehu (reddish) hair. Others had told the Kāula that he should meet Pāʻao. They said that he was friendly and wanted to know more about Hawaiian society. But the Kāula had never felt right in his naʻau about him; something about him was not pono. His naʻau had always proven correct, and it had again. Pāʻao was only spying out the land to conquer it.[6]

The Kāula rushed to the front of his heiau. All eyes were fixed on him as he stood regally at the center of the men in front of ʻIokāne heiau. Seeing the Kāula standing there so calmly gave his people a glimmer of hope as Pāʻaoʼs army surged up the mountain. Feather plumes bristling from the weapons of the approaching warriors and the bright red and yellow feather cloaks and helmets of the chiefs gave the impression of a bronzed wave sparkling with colors sweeping up the hillside. Women and children whimpered and cried out in fear as the crouching and leaping warriors sprang nearer and nearer chanting in unison a fierce war chant interspersed with fearsome war cries. Now they could see the bronzed muscular bodies of the lead warriors, covered in tatau (tattoos). Their muscles, quivering in anticipation of battle and blood, were slick and shimmering with sweat. Deadly weapons, clubs with razor-sharp, sharks-teeth spikes, blades lined with sharks' teeth like the serrated edge of a steak knife that could slash a man to the bone, knives and spears of sharpened Marlin beaks that could puncture right through a man, were all vibrating in the sun, hungry for blood.

Suddenly, three huge warriors exploded from the front lines. The one on the left was about 6 feet 3 inches tall. Although thin and wiry, you could see every strand of his powerful muscles quivering with his fury. He sprang so high in the air in his approach that his feet were higher than most of the men on the other side. He swung a huge war spear that was pointed on one end and had a flattened paddle-like blade on the other with such speed and skill it was a blur about his body that could be heard more than seen. He landed like a cat but slinked smoothly back and forth like a huge lizard, his long tongue flicking in and out of a grotesquely scarred face completely covered in tattoos. His tongue seemed to pant in anticipation of the lapping of their blood; indeed, blood already covered the tongue of his blade.

The warrior on the right seemed to be a six-foot rectangle of solid rock. He had bulging thighs the size of tree trunks and arms the size of a man's waist. Power and confidence exuded from him and crackled from his being like electricity. He swung a huge war club as if it were a twig. The one in the middle was nearly seven feet tall and over 300 pounds of muscle. He, too, sprang forward like a cat, unbelievably fast for a man his size. Half of his body was tattooed completely black, giving the illusion that he was half man and half spirit demon. His eyes bulged wide with demonic fury and unearthly growling spewed from his mouth as did his huge tongue. Periodically, short sudden war cries shot from them like piercing arrows. The Hawaiian warriors hoped the involuntary flinching of their muscles at their sudden cries was not visible to the enemy. The three seemed to sizzle and hiss with demonic fury and power. They did not seem to be human at all, how could one defeat such spirit demons? In truth, they had been dedicated to the war god 'Oro and had sacrificed many of their enemies on his temple altar to increase their mana (spiritual power). And great mana it was; in the spirit they seemed to crackle with electrical fire that created a dark choking cloud filled with the stench of death and terror, piercing the hearts of every man, woman and child on the Kohala side…well, in almost every man.

Suddenly, as if a cool ocean breeze blew back the stifling cloud of darkness, peace and tranquility streamed forth like the rays of the rising sun. Out stepped the Kāula to the front of the men of Kohala. Although white hair flowed from his head, his eyes were filled with fire, the fire of confidence in his God. Although in his seventies now, he calmly stepped out, staff in hand, towards the three imposing warriors towering above him. He may have been old, but his mana had not decreased with age; on the contrary, it had increased. Confusion and then terror inexplicably overwhelmed the warriors, a terror they could not comprehend, a terror they had never felt before. What was this power of the Kāula, a spiritual power and authority from a higher spiritual plane than theirs? What kind of sacrifice could be so much more powerful than their many human ones and what god could be more powerful than 'Oro, the God of War? They had never felt this way in any of their many battles. For the first time, they were the ones hesitating in fear, frozen and unable to move.

The Kāula stopped a few feet directly in front of the middle warrior who seemed to have shrunk significantly. "*Where is your Ali'i Nui (high chief)? Where is your Kahuna Nui (great priest)?*" "*I, the Kahuna Nui of 'Io desire to speak with him!*" A murmuring went up through the crowd of warriors and then shouts and cheers rose from the rear ranks. It seemed as if a huge rolling ball of mana was opening a path through the sea of warriors. A thunderous presence was approaching, nearer and nearer. The Kāula braced for the spiritual impact of the approaching mana. The immense evil of this mana could only come from the Great Sorcerer himself, concentrated in him by thousands of human sacrifices.

It broke like a wave over the people and they fell back involuntarily. Only the Kāula stood firm, as if rooted like a massive tree on an immoveable stone. This great rolling wave of evil seemed to crash directly onto the enormous stone and then was pushed back into the ocean. The two great kahuna nui finally faced one another; it was a moment suspended in time. It seemed as if all creation held its breath as the two men sensed each other's mana and parried in the spirit.

If one's spiritual eyes were open, one would see the cloud of almost audible buzzing spirits swarming around Pā'ao like a cloud of flies. Large dark shadows whooshed back and forth above him. Pā'ao was a tall and powerfully built man. He was very fair and had the reddish blond hair and light eyes of the "Ehu" strain of Polynesians.[7]

Pā'ao's light eyes seemed to turn red with his hatred of the Kāula. He had heard of this man, the "Pono One." And yet for all his overwhelming forces, his eyes flitted about warily with a hint of fear. It wasn't Pā'ao the physical man so much as his demonic array in the spirit that felt the fear. Pā'ao the man felt very cautious because he felt the weakness in his spirit.

A young regal looking man came up next to Pā'ao wearing the royal colors of red and yellow on his feather cape, helmet and *maro* (belt). "This must be Pili, the self-proclaimed new *Ali'i Nui* (high chief)," the Kāula thought cynically.

"*We are taking back this land from the decadent leaders here who do not keep the sacred kapu (taboos) and defile the 'āina!*" Pā'ao spat with a look of disgust at how commoners on the 'Iokane side were standing in the shadows of the ali'i(s). [Hawaiian words are not made plural with an "s." Plural Hawaiian words will be designated by (s) in this book]. This offense was punishable by death. The commoners being so close to the ali'i(s) was debasement of the sacred by the common! Some of the common children were even gripping the legs of their ali'i(s) in their fear. What an open disgusting display of defilement. *"Their blood deserves to be shed!"* Pā'ao thought.

*"It is you who defile this land, Pā'ao, with your human sacrifice and bloodshed for the sake of power and prestige. Man is sacred and his blood is not to be shed! The shedding of innocent blood defiles and pollutes the 'āina!"* the Kāula countered without fear.

Pā'ao looked like he would explode with demonic fury, his fair skin turned crimson. *"Innocent blood! Innocent blood!"* he snarled. *"All of you deserve to have your blood shed upon this land! It is not innocent! You have defiled the sacred kapu!"*

*"Kapu to whom!"* roared the Kāula. His mana was so strong that this one man's voice made the whole army seem to shrink back.

*"To the true God Ta'aroa and his son, 'Oro!"*[8] Pā'ao spat back.

*"Well then take your god Ta'aroa and his son, 'Oro, back to Kahiki (Tahiti) where they will not be offended. We serve 'Io and his Son here."*

*"Who is the son of 'Io?"*

*"His name is Kāne, the Man."*[9]

Pā'ao was livid, he had had enough of this old man who did not respect his sacred person. *"Enough of your babbling old man, I will only give you the same three choices that I have given the other priests of your weak god. If you resist me and continue to worship 'Io, you will die! If you are smart, you will join me as other wise priests of 'Io have, and I will increase your status and power. Or, you can step down, become a lowly maka'āinana (commoner) living in squalor, and never speak of 'Io again. Choose!"* he roared.

The Kāula had already heard of the three choices given to others. But ʻIo had told him what he must do. It would be the most difficult thing the Kāula would ever do, to turn his precious family temple over to the defilements of Pāʻao. If ʻIo himself had not asked him to do it, he would have chosen death. He could not imagine how he would be able to survive anyway. It would be like watching someone rape and defile his precious children and all of his ancestors at the same time! How he wished this dreaded day had never come. There was only one small glimmer of redeeming hope left in him: "The Promise" that someday, far in the future, one of his *pua*, his descendants, would restore his family temple to the worship of ʻIo; the "Pono One" would come. ʻIo promised it and ʻIo never lied!

The Kāula stepped down.

# 4
# The Kapu (Taboo) System

*Historically, religions and truths have often been twisted and changed by unscrupulous leaders to gain personal power and control over people. Throughout history, new "gods" and new doctrines have popped up—concocted by minds bent on the domination and control of others. This was no different in Hawai'i.[1]*

The Kāula wept bitterly as he watched Pā'ao desecrate the sacred grounds of his ancestors. With great ceremony, the Tahitian priest placed bloody stones from Taputapuatea and Waha'ula on the 'Iokāne heiau in direct defiance of 'Io. *"Great 'Io, how could you let this happen? I know you are omnipotent! You could destroy this whole army if you wanted to."* The Kāula struggled to understand the ways of 'Io. All he could do was cling in faith to the prophecy of "The Promise" that someday the defilement would cease, the heiau would be cleansed, and re-dedicated to 'Io. Someday, the "Pono One" would come. But for now all the Kāula could see in his mind's

63

eye was blood—hundreds and eventually thousands of his beloved people being murdered and sacrificed on these temple grounds. Innocent blood would run like a river. He wept bitterly, "Oh, merciful 'Io, please forgive us!"

## After the Death of the Kāula

The kahuna of the 'Iokāne *heiau* demanded action. "*I don't care if no one has broken a kapu, Kū* (the god earlier known as 'Oro[2]) *demands a sacrifice two days from now!*" Kū had to be appeased. It would bring disaster on the community if the ceremony could not be completed. "*Send out the Mū[3] (Professional Executioners) tonight. If they don't find anyone who is breaking a kapu, have them grab anyone and make something up!*"

That night after dark, the Mū slipped out among the huts of the nearby village, listening secretly to conversations around the fires. They listened for any who might complain about the kahuna(s), the ali'i(s), the kapu system or the gods. But no complaint was heard. Surely tomorrow they would find someone to offer as the sacrifice.

---

Kaholowai stood up and stretched his back, surveying with pride the taro fields of North Kohala. Although his people had developed an efficient system of taro farming, it was still back-breaking work. He had spent most of his life standing calf deep in the mud, planting, tending, and harvesting taro. At age 40, Kaholowai knew he was getting old for this kind of labor, but he enjoyed working with his hands in the 'āina and seeing its fruitfulness. He took a long moment to drink in the beauty of the land, sky and sea. Kaholowai smiled, "No, it is not really work when you love the land," he thought. Like all maka'āinana, his was a simple subsistence lifestyle. He raised enough taro to feed his family and to trade for a few fish. For all of the wars, work projects, strict kapu (taboos) and heavy taxes he had suffered at the hands of the ali'i(s) and kahuna(s),[4] he retained his aloha and lived a simple happy life as best he could.

Kaholowai's gaze drifted above him to 'Iokane heiau. He reminisced about when he was a little child and how 'Iokane was once a place of peace, love, and safety. It was now a place of fear and dread. Many innocent Hawaiians had been sacrificed on the altar of 'Iokane since Pā'ao came. Even more had been killed for breaking the kapu(s) he instituted.[5] Yes, there were kapu(s) before his time, but the harsh ones were added *after* Pā'ao. Before he came only good kapu(s) existed—ones used to serve the people and protect the 'āina. For instance, fish were kapu to catch during spawning season. This insured that they would multiply so there would be fish for his children and his children's children.

Now harsh kapu(s) instilled fear in everyone. A man or woman would be killed if one stepped on ali'i land, even if the boundary was not well marked and overgrown! One would be killed if the shadow of an ali'i fell on them. Kaholowai remembered as a child climbing onto the lap of the Kāula, even though he was the kahuna nui! The Kāula had just tickled and hugged him! Now if a child even touched an ali'i, he would be killed immediately. Maka'āinana (common Hawaiian) men were killed for eating certain fish or other foods. Of course the best foods were reserved for the chiefs and priests! Maka'āinana women would be killed for eating bananas, coconuts, pork and many other tasty foods. Mercy was never shown. "*Not true mercy!*" Kaholowai said to himself. He recalled a time when a girl too young to understand the kapu had innocently eaten a banana. The kahuna 'mercifully' spared her life. He just poked out one of her eyes![6]

Many men who had broken a kapu by accident had become human sacrifices at the heiau(s). Their heads lined the walls, stuck on paehumu poles.[7] Sometimes these unfortunate ones were used for bait for shark hunting!

Numerous new gods were also introduced during Pā'ao's time. There was Kanaloa (Ta'aroa),[8] the new line of blood-thirsty Kū gods,[9] ancestor gods like Pele,[10] Kihawahine, Kamapua'a, and many other gods like the Kālaipāhoa gods of sorcery and poisoning. Kaholowai could not keep up with all of the gods. It was so much simpler in the past when he worshipped a great creator God who was too great and holy for any image to be made of him. *"How could one create an image of omnipotence itself?"* How unbelieveable it was to Kaholowai that men would carve images with their own skill and labor, and then worship what they had made. But what could be done now? This new system was already entrenched in Hawai'i; and the ali'i(s), kahuna(s) and their warriors were too powerful for him to do anything about it. The false creator god, Ta'aroa (Kanaloa), through his son, 'Oro (who had morphed into Kū) the god of war, had tightened his tentacles firmly over these precious jewels, the islands of Hawai'i! He must now find lōkahi within himself. Kaholowai looked at the beauty of the 'āina around him and took a deep breath. He was thankful that he had lived in better days. He was thankful too that his family would have enough to eat for another day.

Suddenly Kaholowai realized he had been immersed in the 'āina too long. The sun was setting, and it would be dark soon. *"Auwē!"* he cried. He had to hurry home and prepare the food for the evening meal. Dinner would be late and his children would be hungry and complaining again. He knew carrying his heavy load of taro home down the steep coastline trail would be difficult this late. So impulsively he headed down the shorter and easier trail along the river bed that passed near the Aliʻi(s) kauhale (compound of huts). As Kaholowai rushed down the trail, he did not realize just how near he was to the huts of the Aliʻi(s). Turning a corner on the trail he stopped dead in his tracks. There, coming towards him, was the chief of the ahupuaʻa (a pie-shaped district that ran from the mountains to the sea), Pōhakualiʻi. Pōhakualiʻi was hated by all in the ahupuaʻa. Though he was of high birth, as a chief who was skinny and sickly, he was the brunt of jokes by the other chiefs, so he let his frustration out by "kicking the dog," so to speak. Although Kaholowai had heard of good generous aliʻi(s) in other districts, Pōhakualiʻi was known for his cruelty.

"So, makaʻāinana (commoner), what's in the bag?" Pōhakualiʻi hissed. Kaholowai dropped to the ground and did not raise his eyes. Oh why did he not take the ocean trail home! "It is but a few deformed taro, just enough for my family to stay healthy to serve you better my lord." If Pōhakualiʻi was alone, Kaholowai would be tempted to ring his scrawny neck! But he was never alone; the two large koa (warriors), with the shark's teeth blades standing on either side of him, made Kaholowai keep his eyes down. He was shivering in fear.

He knew well the story about Pōhakualiʻi coming across a young couple on this very same trail, "Damn his stupidity! If only he hadn't been in such a rush and had taken the safer trail!" The young couple was so in love, they too did not see Pōhakualiʻi coming. He had taken a fancy to the beautiful young wife and was going to rape her right on the path. The young husband couldn't control himself and looked up with anger in his eyes. Pōhakualiʻi had walked to the side of the sun so his shadow fell upon him, thus, breaking a kapu. If the shadow of an aliʻi fell on any lowly commoner, that one was killed. Immediately, the koa(s) grabbed the young husband.

One broke his arms and legs with vicious strikes with his club while the other stuck his thumbs in his eyes until they popped out of their sockets. He was then dragged away to the heiau to be that week's sacrifice while his wife screamed in anguish.

Pōhakualiʻi laughed the whole time and then he raped the young man's wife. The thought made Kaholowai more submissive. "But all I have is yours, oh, Great One. Please accept my humble offering." This groveling pleased Pōhakualiʻi very much. He motioned to one of his slaves who quickly grabbed the bag. As Pōhakualiʻi and his entourage moved on, he called back over his shoulder to the koa(s), "Beat him anyway. Let him be thankful that he has his life."

It was well after dark by the time Kaholowai limped home empty handed. Blood dripped from his shoulder where one of the koa(s) had cut his arm for fun with his shark's tooth blade. His wife, Haunani, his son, Manakai, and his little daughter, Wailani, helped him lie down in the little hut. He felt emasculated, being seen like this in front of his wife and children. He had to tell them what happened and why there would be no dinner that night. He could see his wife's hurt, his son's anger and his daughter's fear. The common element in their reactions being a loss of the sense of security a father tries to bring to his family. They felt helpless and fearful. As a man, this made Kaholowai angry.

"If Pōhakualiʻi was alone, I would have choked his scrawny neck! I could do nothing because he had several koa(s) with weapons all around me. I hate him! I will talk to the other men to make a plan to kill him!" Haunani was frightened now, "Kaholowai! Keep your voice down! What if someone hears you? They could tell the kahuna(s) or the aliʻi(s) to gain favors. Please be quiet and rest."

"I remember when I was young, before Pāʻao came. We did not live in fear of the kahuna(s) and aliʻi(s). We did not live *in fear of punishment and death. The Kāula was fair, we were happy and had lōkahi. Life was pono! I wish we could overthrow these new ali'i(s) and go back to the old days when we worshipped the one true God instead of these many cruel ones!"*

It happened in an instant; four huge tattooed men screamed into the hut and held Kaholowai down—the Mū! The little family was in such shock, they were frozen like statues as a fifth man walked in the door and with the skill of a trained executioner, broke Kaholowai's arms and legs with precision strikes from his heavy hardwood club. The loud cracking of Kaholowai's bones sparked screams of agony. The Mū took joy in practicing his art and gleefully took special care to pop out Kaholowai's eyes whole.[11] In another instant, they were gone, dragging Kaholowai to the heiau, his arms and legs flopping helplessly. All the little family could hear was Kaholowai choking on his own blood, and then, it was silent. The only evidence of the Mū was the dark stain of Kaholowai's blood on the dirt floor. Then Wailani began to scream. Nothing could console the little girl. She went into shock. Wailani died of terror and grief that night.

Kaholowai died the next day. He was thrown onto the stone with the holes for the strangling cord to go through it and the grooves to catch the blood and excretions; his arms and legs flopped down helplessly. The cord went over his neck and through the holes in the stone on either side. Then a Mū gleefully pulled the ends of the cords tight, strangling him. Kaholowai's body was washed[12] and then broiled on the sacrificial fire[13] before being placed on the altar of Kū. Haunani failed to stifle her horror as she desperately tried to block out the smell of cooking human flesh that wafted down the valley. Later, when Kaholowai's putrefied flesh melted from his bones, his body was disposed of. But his head was impaled on a paehumu pole; forever to remain a trophy of Kū on the palisades of his heiau.

Wailing in helpless agony at the destruction of her beloved family, Haunani cried out to God, "Oh, *Ke Akua Maoli* (The True God), *the one to who man is sacred. Your law was that man was not to be killed. When will you save us from the Lord of Darkness (Ta'aroa)? When will you remove this evil squid that sucks the life from our beloved islands and its people? Oh, 'Io, e kōkua iā mākou, help us!*"

# 5
# The Kahuna 'Anā'anā

*"Contrary to popular belief, most kahuna(s) weren't bad; the word just meant an expert who had special knowledge. He could be an expert in genealogies, herbal medicines or bone setting. However, the most important kahuna(s), those at the human sacrifice heiau(s), and the kahuna 'anā'anā(s), those practicing black witchcraft, made the word a fearful term."*

The morning sunlight streamed down the Hālawa Valley, one of the most verdant valleys on the island of Moloka'i. Well-ordered lo'i kalo (taro patches) could be seen along the river all the way up the lovely valley. It was a beautiful picture of Hawaiian culture from the volcanic sand at the bay where the fishermen *huki* (pulled) their nets and children caught *'ōpae* (shrimp) at the river mouth, through the well ordered taro patches and fruit trees, and up into the beautiful 'Ōhi'a and Koa forests of the mountain tops. It was paradise indeed!

The idyllic setting was shattered by a piercing command, *"Kulamana! Quickly son, get off of the trail."* The mother of the young boy had been pounding *tapa* (bark cloth) when she saw the kahuna ʻanāʻanā coming up the path. She quickly took her son and all the personal possessions she could carry and hid behind a large rock away from the trail; she dared not even peek at him.

An ominous darkness seemed to precede the kahuna ʻanāʻanā up the trail, like the queasy feeling one gets at the onset of illness. Hunched over, leaning on his walking stick, he walked slowly up the valley. Fear was his power over people. When people feared, it was easy for him to send spirits to overcome them. As he walked, he saw out of the corner of his eyes, the people running and cowering in terror, they did not want to take any chance of offending him. All he needed was something that belonged to them, one of their personal belongings or better yet, some hair, toenails or fingernails. Then his demons, like bloodhounds, could find the victim in the spirit realm. When the victim was asleep, they would entice his soul out of his body and take it to him. He would then entrap it in a gourd. The person's body would soon die.

But this was a special day, a day of great power, a male child was born to his nephew. All first-born male children in his clan belonged to him! He would eat them to retain the mana of his family within him.[1] This cannibalism was a well guarded secret within his family. Whenever he prayed someone to death or sent his demons out to do harm, it cost him dearly of his mana, his life force. Eating a child replaced his mana. He knew his nephew would not want to give up this child, but they had only two choices. They could give up the child to their uncle or he would pray the child to death and curse their family, too. Neither was good, but one choice would cost only one life. No one had ever dared to refuse him.

Mana Kūpuna watched his wife Kuʻulei cradle her precious child. It was their first child. But Mana was not filled with joy at what should be a precious moment, Mana was filled with anguish. He hated his uncle but would never dare to let him know. No good could come from it. He hated his family, "*Why did I have to be born into the Kūpuna family of kahuna ʻanāʻanā?*" He gazed at Kuʻulei, his precious Kuʻulei, how she loved him! Above the objections of her whole family she married him. Her love had made her a fool! She knew the Kūpuna family had a heritage of being kahuna ʻanāʻanā. She had even heard the rumors about the the murder and eating of first-born sons but Mana was so loving and kind to her, she couldn't believe it. She had pushed it out of her mind, but now that dreadful day had arrived. She gazed at Mana full of love and the glow of motherhood. This precious child was the result of their aloha for one another and was theirs alone. She had named the child Makana, meaning "gift,: for he was the precious gift of their aloha.

Mana shivered; it seemed as if a creeping chill had seeped into the cozy hut. A call from the pathway outside startled Mana. "*Huuuui.*" They had had many happy visitors since the birth of their son but Mana sensed a darkness, a pervasive evil. He got up cautiously and peered out of the hut. It took awhile for his eyes to adjust to the darkness, but then his fears suddenly became awful reality.

There in the shadows created by the moonlight outside of his hut stood his uncle. Mana was filled with both fear and anger at the sight of him. "*Aloha e Mana,*" his uncle greeted him. Mana's hackles rose at the sound. "*Aloha, what a hypocrite!*" Mana did not answer, extremely rude; the kahuna only smiled, but his eyes rolled up until you could see only the whites.[2] This shot fear into Mana's soul. When the kahuna ʻanāʻanā were casting curses on someone, this is what they did with their eyes. "*It is time! You know why I am here.*" His uncle growled, stepping forward, the white of his eyes glowing in the moonlight. Mana had contemplated killing his uncle when he came but, after thinking it through, realized that it was futile. The other kahuna ʻanāʻanā(s) in the family would just curse him or even more cruelly, curse Kuʻulei to a wretched painful death! He had seen others who had been cursed by *kahuna ʻanāʻanā*. Some were eaten up from the inside with worms, screaming in agony. Others had their eyes rot and fall out of their heads as the wasting disease ate their bodies alive.[3] He could not even imagine his beautiful Kuʻulei dying like this! An overwhelming fear crept through his bones, sapping his strength away, willing him into resignation and defeat. He turned to the hut a dazed and broken man.

The kahuna ʻanāʻanā walked slowly away from the little hut with the screaming helpless baby in his arms, soon to be his meal. "*Ahhh!*" The more innocent and pure the human life was, the more mana he would gain. He was not in a hurry, he savored the moment. He grinned at the bloodcurdling screams coming from the little hut. "*Scream my dear, scream. Let the whole valley hear and tremble in terror, it only increases my power over them.*"

Kuʻulei never recovered from the shock and horror of that night and died within a few weeks. She was not sick; she died of a broken heart.

"*How much longer, O ʻIo, must this present darkness last!*"

It is always the darkest just before the dawn, but the Sun of Righteousness will soon arise with healing in his wings!

"*Ua kali ahonui aku la au iā Ka Haku, a maliu mai ia me ka hoʻolohe I koʻu hea ʻana!*" "*I waited patiently for the Lord; He inclined to me and heard my cry!*"

*Interlude*

# Hawaiian History
# Between Ancient Hawai'i
# and Modern Times

# 6
# The Return of the True God

*"Let us go to this church and listen to their minister. If it is*
*good and they are right in their teaching about their powerful*
*God of the universe, then we will keep that same God. The*
*reason is that we have a God like theirs. If they are exag-*
*gerating that their God is better than our God, then they are*
*wrong. We Hawaiians have had a powerful and all-knowing*
*God from the beginning and until today."*

—The ancestors of Malia Craver,
who were worshippers of 'Io,
when they met the missionaries

L ike a flickering flame of hope, the 'Iokāne 'ohana carefully
guarded the knowledge of 'Io and the prophecy of "The
Promise." The flame was passed through the generations from
one "Pono One" to the next. If the kahuna of the Kapu System
ever discovered their secret it would mean death! Each link in
the chain of "Pono Ones" kept alive the hope that a special "Pono
One" would arrive soon to restore their precious family heiau to
the worship of 'Io. He would be the One to fan their tiny flame
into a brilliant fire and dispel the darkness in their islands.

Pā'ao's religion of terror lasted until 1819 when it was overthrown by the Hawaiian people themselves. Three Hawaiian

kāula had given prophecies concerning this change prior to the overthrow of the Kapu System. One kāula prophesied the Hawaiian God of Peace (Lono) would return in a new form. He would return in a small black box and speak a language that they would not understand.[1] A generation before the overthrow, another kāula, Kalaikuahulu, said that a communication would be made from heaven by Ke Akua Maoli, the True God.[2] This communication would be entirely different than anything they had ever known. He also prophesied the overthrow of the Kapu System. Another kāula, Kapihe, announced in Kamehameha's presence about three years before he unified Hawai'i that *"The ancient kapu will be overthrown, the heiau and lele altars will be overthrown, and the images will fall down. God will be in the heavens; the Islands will unite, the chiefs will fall, and those of the earth (the lesser people) will rise."*[3]

King Kamehameha unified the islands as prophesied, but he maintained the Kapu System of Pā'ao. When asked by Chief Kuakini why he didn't change the harsh religious practices, especially of human sacrifice, Kamehameha replied, *"You don't think me such a fool as to put any faith in their efficacy. I only suffer them because I find them useful in keeping my people in subjection."*[4] But Kamehameha set in motion the overthrow of the Kapu System by forbidding death companions for himself when he died. By rejecting this practice of killing wives and servants so they could accompany a High Chief into the afterlife, he was defying the old system.

After he passed away on October 3, 1819, two of his wives and his son Liholiho, the new king, broke the kapu as prophesied. Kamehameha's most sacred wife, *Ke'ōpūolani* said, *"Our gods have done us no good; they are cruel."*[5] Hewahewa, the kahuna nui (high priest) of this harsh religious system, was a direct descendant of Pāʻao. Knowing the earlier prophecies, he recognized that a communication from the True God was near. He was the first to burn a heiau of the old gods. Hewahewa said, *"I knew the wooden images of deities, carved by our own hands, could not supply our wants, but worshipped them because it was a custom of our fathers...My thought has always been, there is one only great God, dwelling in the heavens."*[6]

These statements of Kamehameha and Hewahewa, who both knew of ʻIo, confirm that the kahuna and aliʻi knew the ways of the old gods were wrong. This is further displayed by the following story.

When Chiefess Kapiʻolani was a young girl she ate a banana, breaking a kapu because women were not allowed to eat bananas. But because she was a high aliʻi, Kapiʻolani was not put to death. Instead, a kahuna took her favorite servant, a child named Mau, and strangled him on the altar of the heiau. Many years later after the overthrow of the Kapu System, Kapiʻolani asked the kahuna who had strangled her friend Mau why he had done this. The kahuna replied, *"Those were dark days, **though we priests knew better all the time.**"* The kahuna continued, *"**It was power we sought over the minds of the people, to influence and control them.**"* Kapiʻolani hid her face in her hands and wept.[7]

The new king and Kamehameha's favorite wife, Kaʻahumanu, soon initiated sweeping reforms that broke the reign of terror in the islands. The Kapu System was abolished, the heiaus were destroyed and human sacrifice was ended. Hewahewa announced that the new god was coming and went off to await his arrival. The oppressive tentacles of Taʻaroa, the evil-smelling squid, were lifted off the islands. Hawaiʻi was suspended in a spiritual void. If ʻIo did not replace him soon, Taʻaroa, the Prince of Darkness over Polynesia, would soon reassert his claim to the land. Meanwhile, just 20 days after the breaking of the kapu, the first missionaries embarked for Hawai'i by sea, a journey of over 18,000 miles.

These Christians from New England came at the request of a young Hawaiian boy named 'Ōpūkaha'ia, who was later given the English name, Henry. 'Io had preserved Henry through many trials for this very purpose. When he was ten, Henry's village was attacked by enemy warriors. While Henry was fleeing with his younger brother on his back, a warrior threw a spear at them, killing his younger brother. The villagers, including the parents of 'Ōpūkaha'ia, were massacred. But 'Io gave Henry favor with the warrior who speared his brother. He took Henry captive and put him into training to become a kahuna. Henry was taken from his isolated country village to a heiau next to one of the most active trading bays in Hawai'i. This bay was called *Kealakekua*, meaning *the Pathway of God*. It was at this bay that the British explorer, Captain James Cook, arrived 30 years earlier. Since then other ships began arriving to trade.

Meanwhile, 'Ōpūkaha'ia went through rigorous training and had to learn word for word the long chants of the kahuna. He determined to escape and his chance came when he and another young Hawaiian named Hopu swam out to the American whaling ship, Triumph. 'Io gave favor again as the sea captain took both boys on a long voyage to Asia and finally to New England where they arrived in 1809.

As Henry 'Ōpūkaha'ia listened and learned about the world beyond Hawai'i, he developed a thirst for knowledge. One day he was found on the steps of Yale College, weeping because he wanted to learn about God. Again Henry gained favor and was taken in by the president of Yale. Because of his trained mind, Henry learned quickly. In a few years, he mastered English, Greek, Latin and Hebrew and received the equivalent of a Ph.D. degree. He also came to know Jesus and chose to follow him. Henry's example proved extremely important because most Christians of that era believed native peoples (the heathen) could not be educated and, therefore, could not accept Christ. Consequently, there was no formal American mission to native peoples outside the country. Henry changed all of this by proving to be both an exceptional scholar and a committed Christian.

Henry began developing a written Hawaiian language, and translating the scriptures into his native tongue. He also visited churches across New England, pleading for missionaries to go to Hawai'i. But he contracted typhoid fever and died without ever returning to his beloved islands. He became the seed that was planted by God to bear much fruit. Henry's memoirs became the best selling book in New England.[8] This young man of Hawai'i so touched many hearts and minds that the American Board of Commissioners for Foreign Missions was formed to send missionaries to Hawai'i. Henry's example also inspired them to send missionaries to Native Americans and other native peoples.

Although the missionaries left Boston Harbor 20 days after the overthrow of the old religious system in Hawai'i, it took them six months to reach Hawai'i. The missionaries had been praying the whole way over, expecting to face a powerful, entrenched and oppressive religious system. Instead, they rejoiced to find that the Hawaiian people had overthrown their old religious system and were waiting for the True God to be revealed. God had gone before them to prepare the way!

When the missionaries arrived in Hawai'i, they were directed to Kailua on the Big Island where the king resided. Hewahewa had given a prophecy to Liholiho, who took the name King Kamehameha II. He had pointed to a rock on the shore of Kailua Bay and said, *"Here O king, the new God shall come!"* When the missionaries reached Kailua Bay, they landed on the very rock Hewahewa had prophesied over. This rock still remains today and is known as the "Plymouth Rock of Kona."[9] It lies under the pier next to the King Kamehameha Hotel in Kailua-Kona.

One old Hawaiian prophecy said the true God would return in a form they would not recognize and another said the god of peace would return in a small black box and speak a language they would not understand. The first missionary stepped onto "Plymouth Rock" carrying a small black box. Because they were hand pressed, Bibles were highly valued. Special boxes were made to protect them, especially on long voyages. When the box was opened by the king, the book inside (the Bible) contained a strange language they could not understand. Various kahuna then proclaimed that the Hawaiian God of Peace had returned in his new form. The new God, the true God of the Hawaiian people, 'Io had returned as prophesied!

It was the last high priest of the old religion, Hewahewa, a descendant of Pā'ao, who prophesied where the new God would arrive and it was Hewahewa who composed a chant to welcome the new God.

*"Arise, stand up, stand, fill up the ranks, stand in rows, stand lest we be in the darkness, in the black of night, Ye thorny hearted, assembled, a multitude, stand, A great God, a mighty God. A living God, an everlasting God is Jehovah, a visitor from the skies; a God dwelling afar off, in the heights, At the further end of the world, in the rolling cloud, floating in air. A light cloud resting on the earth, a rainbow standing in the ocean, in Jesus, our redeemer. By the past from a foreign land to us in Hawai'i he*

*comes from zenith to the horizon a mighty rain from the heavens, Jehovah the supreme, we welcome."*[10]

The True Hawaiian God, 'Io, also known as 'Ia and 'Iaonalaninuiamamao ('Ia of the great and distant heavens) had returned. *"Sing unto God, sing praises to his name: extol him that rideth upon the heavens by his name JAH, and rejoice before him"* (Psalm 68:4 KJV). Hallelujah literally means Praise Jah!

# 7
# The Great Awakening

*"With all their deficiency of candor, humor, and common sense, the missionaries are the best and most useful whites in the Pacific."[1]*

—Robert Louis Stevenson

When the American missionaries began preaching the Gospel in Hawai'i in the 1820s, they were approached by several families who worshipped 'Io. These families recognized their benevolent Creator was the same as Jehovah. However, they told the missionaries they knew of Jehovah by another name, 'Io or 'Ia. Here, the missionaries made their first of a series of mistakes by telling these families that Jehovah was not the same as "their heathen god." Some Hawaiians were confused by this, but at least two families knew in their hearts that 'Io and Jehovah were the same. They continued to secretly worship Jehovah and 'Io as one.

One of these families was that of Hewahewa;[2] the other was the 'Iokāne family.

Most of the missionaries, by their selfless love and sacrifice, helped turn the hearts of the Hawaiian people toward Christ. The years between 1837 and 1850 would become known as "Hawai'i's Great Awakening" when thousands came to accept Iesū Kristo (Jesus Christ), and Hawai'i became 96 percent Christian! Two key figures in this Great Awakening that began in Hilo, Big Island (Hawai'i) and spread to all of the Hawaiian Islands were Kapi'olani, a high ali'i who had become a Christian, and Titus Coan, a fiery American evangelist. Kapi'olani turned the hearts of her people to Christ by defying the feared volcano goddess Pele. She marched into the very jaws of the active volcano, Kīlauea, to show that Jehovah was more powerful than Pele and the true God of the volcano. Later, multitudes received Christ as Coan traveled throughout the Hilo and Puna districts of the Big Island declaring the gospel of salvation by faith. Coan's church, Haili, in Hilo became the largest church in the world with 10,000 people attending services in that town of only 1,000 people! The phenomenon was described as a ten-year continuous camp meeting.

It was reported about this time that, "*One could scarcely go in any direction, in the sugar cane or banana groves without finding children praying and weeping before God.*"[3]

The missionaries, with their strong Protestant work ethic, labored tirelessly to establish schools, medical clinics and churches throughout the islands. They continued translating the Bible and other books into Hawaiian and taught the people to read and write in the Hawaiian language. They also battled the negative influences of foreigners who introduced drunkenness, gambling and prostitution to the islands. Many historians agree that, if the missionaries had not greatly reduced prostitution and vaccinated the Hawaiian people against small pox, venereal diseases and small pox could have wiped out the Hawaiian population. Even author Mark Twain, who was often critical of piously religious people, praised the missionaries for improving the lot of the common people of Hawai'i.[4] Many of the missionaries died penniless after a life of service to the Hawaiian people. Despite their hard work and noble intentions, they made several critical mistakes that, decades later, served to quench the Christian movement in Hawai'i.

The Great Enemy of our souls is not a creator. He can only corrupt, lie about and steal what has already been created. Although every culture has been corrupted and contains evil elements that were "grafted into it," the root and core of the culture was created by God for His good purposes. Many missionaries rejected the Hawaiian culture outright, indiscriminately dismissing it as completely evil. By contrast, the missionaries viewed their New England culture as the only acceptable expression of true Christianity and Hawaiian converts were expected to adopt their lifestyle—to act and dress—like white New Englanders. This emulation of a foreign culture, this *putting on an act,* created a dichotomy in the Hawaiian psyche of not being real before God, thus causing a creeping conflict in the souls of Christian Hawaiians. If they had to culturally mimic the "White Man" to be accepted by God, did the White Man's God really love Hawaiians? It was the wedge the Dark Lord of Polynesia, Ta'aroa, would use to pry open Hawaiian souls to Him.

# 8
# The Prince of Darkness Returns

*"Let me again fraternally warn you not to be 'greedy of filthy lucre,' and not to do what may even seem to be taking lands on speculation…A sanctified common sense will easily draw the line between proper and improper investments; but let no one trust solely to his own judgment in such a case. I never yet knew a heart, that I felt sure was not capable of great self-deception …"[1]*

—The Secretary of the Mission Board's repeated warning to retiring missionaries

The Mission Board forbade workers from engaging in business transactions for personal gain. All monies earned were to be turned over to the mission. For ethical reasons, missionaries were required to resign from the mission before getting involved in business or politics.[2]

Unfortunately, some former missionaries and their descendants began to accumulate land and money in unethical ways, not following the teachings of the Bible. At the same time, a succession of Hawaiian kings left the worship of the true Creator. They were enticed by Western luxuries, liquor, gambling and vices until the Hawaiian Kingdom was overwhelmed by debt to foreigners.

The last Hawaiian king, Kalākaua, was warned by a minister and kāula, James Ka'uhane, that if he did not repent and return to Jesus, the Hawaiian kingdom would be lost.[3] The Lord of Darkness, Ta'aroa, the evil-smelling squid, worked patiently, on both the former missionaries and the Hawaiian royalty, slowly prying apart the oyster that held the precious pearl of Hawai'i.

The death blow fell on January 17, 1893. On that day, a few missionary descendants with active backing from the U.S. foreign minister and a company of Marines, forced the Christian Queen, Lili'uokalani, to yield, thus overthrowing the Hawaiian Kingdom. Like the Kāula some 700 years earlier when facing the overwhelming forces of Pā'ao, Queen Lili'uokalani, facing the overwhelming power of the United States, stepped down peacefully as ruler of Hawai'i to avoid the senseless bloodshed of her people; both believing in faith that if they did what was pono, God, in His perfect time, would make things pono again for her people.[4]

The Queen appealed to President Grover Cleveland and to the U.S. Congress. Cleveland agreed the overthrow was illegal and refused appeals of the new Hawai'i government to make it a U.S. territory. However, the United States did not use its power to force the usurpers to return the Hawaiian Kingdom to its rightful ruler.

In an appeal for justice to the American Christians, Lili'uokalani wrote, "*Oh, honest Americans, as Christians hear me for my downtrodden people! Their form of government is as dear to them as yours is precious to you. Quite as warmly as you love your country, so they love theirs. With all your goodly possessions, covering a territory so immense that there yet remain parts unexplored, possessing islands that, although new at hand, had to be neutral ground in time of war, do not covet the little vineyard of Naboth's, so far from your shores, lest the punishment of Ahab fall upon you, if not in your day, in that of your children, for "be not deceived, God is not mocked." The people to whom your fathers told of the living God, and taught to call "Father," and whom the sons now seek to despoil and destroy, are crying aloud to Him in their time of trouble; and He will keep His promise, and will listen to the voices of His Hawaiian children lamenting for their homes."*[5]

At the time of the overthrow, the church of the first missionaries was still the dominant Christian church in Hawai'i. It was also the church of the Queen. Even after 73 years in Hawai'i, the Great Awakening, and the vast majority of Hawaiians being Christians, the church board was made up completely of white foreigners. This board immediately endorsed the new government.

During its seven decades in Hawai'i, this church founded by the first missionaries had grown increasingly influential. It had largely rejected Hawaiian culture as "evil" and imposed its own New England, commerce-based culture upon Hawaiians. Despite the pain of losing much of their Hawaiian identity, the vast majority of the Hawaiian people stayed true to the church. They stayed even when it became obvious that some unscrupulous members of the church were taking control of Hawaiian lands through theft and deceit. But the overthrow of their Christian Queen and the stealing of their entire nation of Hawai'i was more than the Hawaiian people could bear. The census of 1853 recorded that Hawai'i was the most Christian nation on earth with 96 percent claiming to be Christian. After the overthrow of Lili'uokalani and the endorsement of the new government by the church board in 1893, an estimated 97 percent of Christian Hawaiians left the church in protest.[6]

The Lord of Polynesia, Ta'aroa, used his tentacles of greed and lust for power to capture the minds and hearts of former servants of God and the Hawaiian royalty to again twist his tentacles down and claim dominance over Hawai'i.

In the late 1700s a kāula named Ka'opulupulu prophesied that white men would become rulers of Hawai'i, the native population would live landless like fishes of the sea, the line of chiefs would come to an end, and a stubborn generation would succeed them who would cause the native race to dwindle.[7] The prophecy of Ka'opulupulu proved true in all points. Still, through all this adversity, God—'Io, who is Jehovah—preserved a faithful remnant of true followers of Iesū, Jesus. Again only a thin thread of faith remained. The 'Iokāne family secretly continued to worship Jehovah and 'Io as one.

After Grover Cleveland left office, Hawai'i became a territory of the United States in 1898—over the protest of almost every Hawaiian family. Decades of despondency and spiritual darkness followed for many Hawaiian people.

Then on December 7, 1941, Pearl Harbor was attacked by the Japanese and Hawai'i was swept into World War II. When war ended in 1945, two generations of 'Iokānes had passed since the overthrow of the Hawaiian Kingdom.

In 1959, Hawai'i became the 50th state of the United States of America. Still the 'Iokānes waited for the special One to be revealed; that special Pono Child who would fulfill "The Promise," and restore their priesthood and their precious heiau to the worship of 'Io.

They wouldn't have to wait long, for the "Promised One" was already born.

Part Two
# The Stage Is Set

# 9
# Moke

"What may be known about God is plain to men because God has made it plain to them. For since the creation of the world God's invisible qualities—His eternal power and divine nature—have been clearly seen, being understood from what has been made [creation around us], so that men are without excuse."

—Romans 1:20 NIV

In 1957, a branch of the 'Iokāne family living on the Big Island welcomed a son into the family. His parents named him Moke. This branch of the 'Iokānes lived in a Hawaiian Homestead called "Keaukaha" in Hilo on the northeast side of the Big Island. Hawaiian homesteads are, in some ways, similar to Native American reservations. It was a well-known homestead that several popular Hawaiian songs had been written about over the years. It was here that Moke grew up.

Like many Hawaiian families in the 1960s, the 'Iokāne family spent its summers camping at the beach—not just for a few days, but <u>all</u> summer. There was no better time to be

a Hawaiian boy than this. Moke and his ʻohana would fish,
dive, swim, surf and play games all day and they would sing,
hula and play Hawaiian music long into the night.

———

Moke's grandfather and patriarch of the family, Iokepa,
waited in his usual spot, a perch on the rocks above a calm
ocean pool in a little bay created by volcanic lava. Everyone
in Keaukaha knew this was Iokepa's spot. The waters of this
pool ran cold because of the fresh water spring that flowed up
into the pool through cracks in the lava rocks below. Iokepa
would stand there as if he were a part of his rock, not only
still physically, but spiritually. His mind did not race with the
cares of this world but rested, every fiber of his mind, body
and soul, just existing totally there on that rock in God's
creation. Iokepa did not seek the trappings of this world; he
desired the lōkahi triangle.

The lōkahi triangle, when all was pono and in perfect balance; when one was right with God, his fellow men, and the
ʻāina (the land, sea, sky and the flora and fauna that live in
it); that special place immersed in God's aloha. Lōkahi meant
unity, peace and harmony. When Iokepa entered the lōkahi
triangle, even though he didn't look like his rock, he seemed
part of the landscape, a part of creation that belonged right
there. When you looked at that spot, you expected to see
Iokepa there.

Iokepa would stand there sometimes all day just observing and appreciating creation as it revolved around him. He
arrived before sunrise to watch the grey sky blossom into
a golden orange and to listen to the different birds as they
sang their praises to ʻIo. He would observe the various fish
below him as they went about their morning feeding. Every
day brought a new canopy of sights, colors, scents, sounds

and feelings, no two days were alike; no two minutes were the same! The canopy of light and color changed slowly, like a giant kaleidoscope with not only changing colors but varying scents, sounds and feelings as the world revolved around Iokepa on his rock from morning to night and from season to season. He would stand on his rock through burning heat and pouring rain, in blustery winds and crashing waves or gentle sea breezes and glassy seas. The universe and all its creation was, in a way, coaching him, sometimes in the soft whisper of gentle island breezes and sometimes in the roaring waves. Listen! They are all the voice of 'Io![1]

'Io spoke to Iokepa like he spoke to another indigenous seeker of God named Job. Most Bible scholars agree that Job was a contemporary of Abraham because of the culture he lived in. Job, therefore, was not a Hebrew. So how did Job come to know God? Job 12:7-10 KJV says, *"But ask the animals, and they will teach you, or the birds of the air, and they will tell you; or speak to the earth, and it will teach you, or let the fish of the sea inform you. Which of all these does not know that the hand of the Lord has done this? In His hand is the life of every creature and the breath of all mankind."*

Like Job, God educated Iokepa through creation. People who do not understand this would think a man like Iokepa was lazy. Some would surely say, *"Why doesn't he make something of his life? Does he have no dreams to fulfill? Does he not want to get somewhere in life?"* Such people fail to consider the countless men and women through the centuries who have gone out to solitary places to hear the voice of God. And on that rock, Iokepa was communing with the Living God!

Some days, Iokepa would stand on the rock all day and never throw his net. Most of the children would become bored with this kind of fishing and run off and play. But Moke often stayed to listen to his grandfather's wisdom, asking many questions. On one of those days, Moke and his tūtū kāne (grandfather) were standing on the rock for a long time. Moke began to get restless and asked, "*How much longer must we stay here, tūtū!*" Iokepa replied, "*What was that Moke? Are you complaining?*" "*No, tūtū, I am sorry.*" Tūtū then began to fold up his net and prepare to leave. "*Are we leaving, tūtū?*" asked Moke, "*But you didn't even throw your net. We didn't catch any fish.*" Tūtū replied, "*I have caught my fish.*" Some 30 years later Moke finally understood what tūtū meant by those words. Moke passed his grandfather's test as the "Pono One" for his generation. Moke was chosen by tūtū kāne to receive the knowledge of 'Io, and he would be the keeper of this knowledge for the family.

From that day forward, Iokepa taught his grandson about the ways of 'Io. Tūtū kāne told Moke that this was their special secret and he was to tell no one. It was not formal schooling like in the Western world or esoteric knowledge, secret signs, and rituals like some secret society; it was very simple, as simple as a grandfather teaching his grandson about life. Tūtū explained that the symbol of 'Io is the Hawaiian hawk; the highest flying and most powerful bird in the islands. This is why the name of the Hawaiian hawk is also 'Io. The *kaona*, the deep inner meaning of 'Io, the hawk, has always been the great Creator who sees and knows all.[2]

Tūtū told Moke one day as they stood together on tūtū's rock, "*See how the hawk flies so high in the sky. From his perch in the sky, he can see the clouds that brush against the mountain peaks and fall as rain. He can see as the rain forms small rivulets that flow into streams. The streams then form rivers, rough rapids and cascading waterfalls, and finally large rivers which flow into the great ocean. Moke, so 'Io can see the stream of your life from beginning to end!*" Tūtū taught Moke many other things about 'Io and His creation. His way of observing and explaining natural things was so simple that Moke often didn't realize he was being taught.

There were no esoteric teachings, difficult incantations or chants to remember; it was learning to have a relationship with his God. It was more like grandfather was leading him through an experience than teaching him facts or concepts. Once Moke's relationship with his God was pono, all things would flow from it. This is the difference between learning about swimming and actually swimming. It's the difference between the Pharisees knowing the laws of God, and Jesus saying if you love God and your neighbor, everything will fall into place. To know a religious system is good; to know the creator of the system is better. If in the beginning there was only God, then all things are made and sustained by His substance and power. If God created all things, then His mana, his spiritual essence, should be in all things. Like a painter leaving his essence, heart and soul in a painting, God's love for us is reflected in His creation. He can be found there! Moke learned no pat answers to anything, just how to know the Creator's heart through what He had made. Principles of *pono* living took deep root in Moke's heart, some of which he would understand only many years later.

A few times Tūtū had told Moke, "You're 'The One.'" When Moke asked Tūtū what he meant by that, Tūtū just said, "*You will find out.*" When Moke grew up and got married, Tūtū told Moke's wife, Pali, several times, "*Moke's 'The One.'* Pali would reply, "*Yes, I know he is the one for me.*" Tūtū would reply, "No, he is 'The One.' Someday you will understand."

Moke's grandfather grew old and died. Although Moke kept his secret, in time, Moke slipped away from his relationship with 'Io.

Moke became a songwriter, musician and a Hawaiian sovereignty activist. At that time, more Hawaiians were homeless or living below poverty level than any other ethnic group in Hawai'i. Even though this was a *pono* cause, the fight to correct the injustices to his people slowly changed Moke. They say if you put a frog in a pot and slowly turn up the heat, he will not even know he is being cooked until it is too late. Ta'aroa, the enemy of 'Io, slowly slipped his tentacles into Moke's life; eventually poisoning Moke's mind and heart and turning him into an angry and bitter man. He eventually fell into drug and alcohol abuse, which nearly destroyed his marriage and family. But through the remnant of Hawaiian Christians, Moke found peace in Iesū Kristo (Jesus Christ), and accepted Him as his Lord and Savior. Moke began attending a church in Keaukaha, but his relationship with 'Io was still placed on the back burner of his mind.

That's when Moke met Daniel.

# 10
# Daniel and Akea

*"E hea i ke kanaka e komo maloko;*
*e hānai ai a hewa ka waha."*
*"Call to the person to enter;*
*feed him until he can take no more."*
—An Old Hawaiian Proverb of Hospitality

Daniel Kikawa took a long time to learn things. As a boy, he loved surfing and martial arts, but it took him five years before he was even average at either of them and seven years before things really started to click. It wasn't until several years after running a branch of his teacher's martial arts school that everything finally came together for Daniel in martial arts. He had to practice and practice before the simplest technique would become natural for him. But that was just the way Daniel was. He was always the plodding tortoise and never the speedy hare.

Daniel eventually became a minister and writer. His slow but steady way is probably why the Lord chose him to be a writer.

Whenever Daniel wrote an article or ministry report, he might revise it 40 times, musing over every sentence. His favorite hero (after Jesus) was Thomas Edison. This legendary inventor was nearly dropped from school because his teacher thought he was retarded. Edison discovered the right light bulb filament after trying thousands of combinations of metals. Others had tried but stopped after trying several hundred. Daniel's favorite saying from Edison was, "*Genius is one percent inspiration and ninety-nine percent perspiration.*" Whenever Daniel accomplished anything in his life, this was how he did it.

Daniel was born and raised in Hawai'i. His grandfather, he was told, was from a wealthy samurai family. His grandfather did not support the Sino-Japanese War so he gave his inheritance to his sisters and left to make his fortune in Hawai'i. Daniel never found out if that story was true. All he knew was that his family had been in Hawai'i for over 100 years. Even so, Daniel was of Japanese ancestry and not considered to be a "real" Hawaiian.

Most people from outside the islands never truly understand the complex layers of culture in Hawai'i. A *malihini* (visitor) would probably only experience the "plastic" Hawai'i. To make this plastic Hawai'i, developers first bulldoze the real Hawai'i and then create fake waterfalls and scenes that portray a fantasy; a false romantic vision of Hawai'i. Most visitors never get past this plastic wrapping (most don't want to), and if they do, many times they are rudely surprised.

The next layer of culture is that of those who recently moved from the "mainland" because they loved the plastic wrapping. Many of them never desire to know what is beneath it. They live in Hawai'i but move and live in their own communities of transplanted mainlanders. They can live here the rest of their lives and never know anything else but their wealthy enclaves associating with only one another.

Next is the "local" culture. Locals are also called *kama'āina* (native born). All Native Hawaiians are *kama'āina* and local but not all kama'āina or locals are Hawaiian. Local culture is very different than Hawaiian culture. While Hawaiian culture is its base, local culture includes elements of *haole* culture (American culture) plus the cultures of the peoples who came as plantation workers, mainly the Portuguese, Chinese, Japanese, Koreans and Filipinos. Local culture is ever expanding to assimilate the cultures of newer immigrants to Hawai'i like Samoans, Tongans, Micronesians, Vietnamese and Thai. When the plantation workers came to Hawai'i in the late 1800s, they all spoke their own languages. To communicate with one another and the Hawaiians and the *haoles* (whites), a unique form of "pidgin" developed out of necessity. Most locals could speak decent English, but when they talked to one another, they used pidgin. Their accent could get so thick and the words come out so fast, that an English speaker would not have a clue what language they were speaking.

A few transplants do become accepted as locals; actually, it's not hard to do. The most important thing is to love, appreciate and learn from the amazing rainbow of cultures and people God brought to Hawai'i. If one comes to Hawai'i with a humble heart and truly loves, appreciates, respects and accepts locals, the locals will accept you even if you can't speak proper pidgin! It takes many years to get the pidgin accent right, and getting your heart right is more important than getting the accent right.

The deepest level of culture in Hawai'i is Native Hawaiian culture. Although Daniel was thoroughly local, growing up he never came to understand Native Hawaiian culture. A local person can spend all of his or her life in Hawai'i and never get to know this level of Hawaiian culture, just like Mainlanders who never knew or understood local culture. Unfortunately, even many Hawaiians do not learn their own native culture.

Daniel finally learned the ways of Hawaiian culture from the Eaton 'ohana. Papa Eaton was three-quarters Hawaiian and was from the family of Princess Ruth Keʻelikōlani. His dad was half Hawaiian and half English, and that is where they got the Eaton name. Mom Eaton was full Hawaiian and grew up speaking Hawaiian as a first language. Daniel became a part of this family when he moved to Maui in 1974.

He was 19, and it was the time of the "Bruce Lee boom." When his teacher proposed that Daniel and his friend Kenny open a martial arts school for him on Maui, Daniel thought, *"Cool, there are great waves on Maui."* So he went. One day, Daniel was interviewing prospective students. As each came in, he noticed how well-dressed, respectful and punctual they were. When the time for the next interview came, he saw the name Eaton and assumed it was some *haole* guy. Daniel would joke later that he should have known it was a Hawaiian because he showed up late, on what locals called "Hawaiian time." As Daniel sat waiting, he heard what sounded like a tank coming down the road. A beat-up Chevy (that used to be white) with a broken muffler and a surfboard on top pulled into the parking lot. The door groaned loudly as it opened revealing a large, well-built Hawaiian man with a sun-bleached semi-afro and reflecting sunglasses. He emerged from the car and pulled on an old T-shirt. He walked in and plopped himself in a chair, dressed for the interview in a faded T-shirt (with a hole in it) and surf shorts. His slippers (flipflops) and feet were full of sand. Akea Eaton couldn't have looked and acted more different than the interviewees who preceded him. Daniel had seen his type before. They were the ones who hung out in the bathrooms at school, doing drugs and hijacking students for their money. The first thing he said to this man was, *"You know, we don't want any troublemakers here."*

That's when Akea realized he had been stereotyped and needed to set things straight with this guy. He took off his "reflecto" glasses so Daniel could see he was not high, and began to "talk story" with him. It was good for Daniel that Akea was older (age 25) and more mellow now. If he had said that to Akea a few years before, they would have probably gotten into a "beef" right there and chances were really good that Akea would have beaten the living daylights out of Daniel. Akea was not only twice Daniel's size, he was an experienced street fighter who had been the "bull" of 'Ewa Beach when he was growing up. 'Ewa Beach was a tough local area, mostly Hawaiian at the time. Later Daniel would find out that Akea had the fastest hands he had ever seen in a big man. A little guy often has only one advantage in a fight with a bigger man—his speed. Akea being so big and fast just seemed unfair. A lightning quick jab from Akea had knocked out many a man when Akea worked as a nightclub bouncer.

Daniel found he was talking to a highly intelligent and thoughtful man, not what his initial impression was at all. Akea had gone to Kamehameha School, a respected school system for children of Hawaiian ancestry, and had gone to college on the Mainland on a football scholarship. He probably would have been playing pro ball if he hadn't blown out his knee. Akea invited Daniel and Kenny to go surfing and camping with him in Hana. Daniel loved to surf at little-known, uncrowded spots so he immediately agreed. That trip would be the start of his Hawaiian education. On the long and beautiful road to Hana, Akea started teaching him about Hawaiian history and traditions, Hawaiian thinking and ways of doing things, and the reason so many Hawaiians were bitter and angry. Akea had learned much by sitting under not only his knowledgeable grandparents and parents but many well-known kūpuna who sensed something about him and had made a special effort to teach him. He was a wealth of knowledge; and for some reason, he felt led to pass his knowledge on to Daniel even though he was not family and not even Hawaiian. Akea and his family spiritually hanai(ed), adopted, Daniel and Daniel began to learn from Mom Eaton also.

Since then, Daniel had been spiritually hānai(ed), adopted, not formally but informally by other Hawaiian families. He had been told by many kūpuna that he was Hawaiian. He remembered Aunty Malia Craver, one of the most celebrated living kūpuna in Hawaii, telling him, *"Don't say you are not Hawaiian anymore. You are Hawaiian because you have a Hawaiian heart."* But although Daniel had come to love and respect the Hawaiian people and their culture as his own, he knew that because he had not grown up in the culture, there were some things he would never fully understand. He would always need the guidance and mentoring of people like Akea. On the other hand, because he was deprived as a child of this culture that he grew to love so much, he drank in whatever he found of the culture like a man dying of thirst and searched for its wisdom like precious pearls.

Daniel had no clue why God had him meet Akea and learn about Hawaiian culture, but he was soon to find out.

# 11

# Aloha Ke Akua (God Is Love)

## 'Io-mata-wai: 'Io, the God of love

*"For God so loved the world, that He gave His only begotten Son, that whosoever believeth in Him should not perish, but have everlasting life."*

—John 3:16 KJV

In 1992, three guys were sitting in a garage in a neighborhood of Kāneʻohe, Oʻahu, "talking story." Hawaiians like to be outdoors in the fresh air and seeing God's creation as much as possible. In the Hawaiian community, you are much more likely to see a picnic table and chairs in the garage than a car; you could call it the Hawaiian patio. The three men were talking story about how to share with the Hawaiian people that God really loved them despite all the wrongs they suffered at the hands of Christians.

The three men were Kawika Kahiapo, Leon Siu and Daniel Kikawa. Kawika was one of the best kīhōʻalu (Hawaiian slack key) guitarists in the islands. He was quite well known in the Hawaiian music world and played guitar for several Hawaiian music legends. He is one of the few full-blooded Hawaiians left. He was also an accomplished songwriter, singer and artist. Leon Siu was one half of the well-known Hawaiian music duo, *Leon & Malia*. He had not only won international awards for his music, but was recognized as an astute political strategist and organizer, and one who was at the vanguard of the Hawaiian cultural renaissance of the 1960s and '70s. Leon was also known by almost everyone in the Hawaiian community. And Daniel, well, Daniel didn't have a clue why he was there with men of such stature.

The idea of *Aloha Ke Akua*, which eventually grew into a full-time ministry for all three men, was birthed in that garage. It was not really an organization, just a loose affiliation of three like-minded people.

As Daniel was praying about how to show the Hawaiian people Jesus really loved them, the Lord showed him that there were three "cords" binding the Hawaiian people from Him. A hungry man may want the food placed in front of him very badly; but if he is bound, he cannot get to it. God showed Daniel that the three "cords" were: 1. Their perception that the God of the Bible was a foreign god, not their God. They wanted a God who loved their people and had cared for them throughout their long history, not a God who lived somewhere else and just recently decided to come to the Hawaiians. 2. They wanted a God who loved who they were, not one who hated their culture and would only love them if they became like "white men." 3. They were hurt by people they thought were true Christians, and so they felt that it was Jesus who hated them and hurt them.

This revelation clarified for the three men their purpose: to break these three cords over the Hawaiian people and other native people like them. The ministry now had a clear vision, and it began moving forward with a purpose.

Daniel's research became a book published by the ministry in 1993 called *Perpetuated in Righteousness*. In the end, the book had taken him eight years of poring through books, searching through libraries and archives, and interviewing kūpuna. *Perpetuated in Righteousness* was written with the guidance of Akea, Kawika, Leon and many of Daniel's hanai 'ohana and kūpuna. Kūpuna like Mom Eaton and Aunty Malia Craver would share things with Daniel that few knew about, sometimes not even their families and close friends. Daniel knew that this was because God was giving him favor with them, but also because he wanted to learn. One day Mom Eaton was teaching Daniel when Akea interrupted saying, "*Mom! How come you neva told me this stuff?*" Mom replied, "*Because you neva ask!*" The book educated thousands of Christians and became a must-read for church leaders and new pastors from the mainland.

God also told Daniel as he was writing *Perpetuated in Righteousness*, "Tell them (the Hawaiian people) that I am 'Io." At that time, most Hawaiians had never heard of that name. Although Aunty Malia Craver and the Eaton 'ohana knew about him, few others Daniel talked with did. One could read a hundred books on Hawaiian history and never come across that name. Daniel did as God directed him and people eventually "came out of the woodwork" to confirm the existence of 'Io. Because of Pā'ao's order that anyone talking about 'Io would be killed, knowledge of 'Io was passed to one trustworthy person in each generation, "The Pono One," under strict orders of secrecy. To reveal knowledge of 'Io meant death. After 800 years of this threat, people forgot the real reasons for the secrecy. It became a superstitious belief that if a person spoke of 'Io, he would die of a curse for breaking this "kapu." Daniel had been told later by one person that they were waiting to see if he would die. When he didn't die, they realized it was okay to come forward to share; after all, the secret was out already.

As the three men and their families did what God told them to do, Aloha Ke Akua's meetings of the three men informally sitting in a garage asking God what to do next eventually turned into big informal gatherings in backyards, garages or beaches on every island. They eventually had a large support group of devoted, thankful friends who had broken free from the three cords and had come joyfully to Jesus. They called this group the "Aloha Ke Akua 'Ohana."

Daniel became an ordained minister and finished his degree in Bible College in good timing because the ministry became a full-time job. In 1995, the Lord told Daniel to move to the Big Island. Kahu Gaymond Apaka invited him to share at their church camp and it was the first place he spoke after his move. Daniel naturally shared what the Lord had told him, "*Tell my Hawaiian people that I am the same as 'Io.*" He had no idea that Moke was in the audience; or that Moke was upset that Daniel knew about 'Io!

While Daniel was sharing, Moke went up to Kahu Apaka and said, "*Who is this guy and how does he know about 'Io?*" At the end of Daniel's talk, Moke stood up and said, "*I am shocked that you know about 'Io. I was taught about 'Io but I thought it was a secret between my grandfather and me. I didn't know anyone else knew about 'Io.*" Although Moke started out angry, Daniel and Landa became friends with Moke and his wife, Pali, as they attended Kahu Apaka's fellowship together.

None of them had a clue as to where this relationship would lead or what the Lord had in store for them.

Part Three
# The 'Io Project

# 12

# The 'Io Project Begins

*"That the Marquesan Tanaoa and the Hawaiian Kanaloa
[the Marquesan and Hawaiian names for the Tahitian
Ta'aroa] embody the same original conception of evil, I consider pretty evident."*

—Hawaiian Historian Abraham Fornander

*"So you shall not pollute the land where you are; for blood
defiles the land."*

—Numbers 35:33a NKJV

Daniel had been researching Hawaiian history for over
eleven years. He had read hundreds of books, combed
through libraries, museums and archives, and spoken with
many kūpuna. From this research he could see a continuing spiritual influence of the malevolent Lords of Darkness,
Ta'aroa and 'Oro. A kahu he deeply respected, Ken Kekoa,
sought out Daniel to convey what the Lord had told him
about this influence. Kahu Kekoa had been asking God
why the old principalities and powers of the Kapu System
were still lords over Hawai'i when the luakini (human sacrifice) heiau(s) had been destroyed. The Lord answered him,

*"Because the blood of the human sacrifices has not been cleansed by the blood of Jesus."*

When Daniel heard this, the Spirit of God within him immediately confirmed it was true. The innocent blood of thousands of Hawaiians sacrificed to Ta'aroa and 'Oro still remained on the land, defiling it and polluting it. This blood had never been cleansed from the land. Consequently, according to Deuteronomy 28, a Biblical curse remained upon the land and the Hawaiian people. God gave to man, made in His image, the stewardship of His creation. If man willingly bows down and worships another god, he has then turned his sovereignty of the land over to the new god he worships! Until man repents of his sin towards God and God forgives his sin, this new god continues to have rights to the land! This meant that Ta'aroa and 'Oro, disguised as the Hawaiian god Kū, still had sovereignty over the land! If they were thrown off for a season by the prayers of men, they had the right to return to the land when the prayers waned. It was like trying to throw off the tentacles of a giant octopus where it had suctioned down in many places. It would take great strength to just unfasten one sucker. Keeping the giant tentacles up off the land would be impossible to do for long.

With all of the prayers going up during the "Great Awakening" some tentacles were thrown off. However, because of his right to the land through the defilement of human blood, the revival began to wane within ten years and Ta'aroa's heavy tentacles suctioned back down solidly by 1893 when the Hawaiian kingdom was overthrown. The land still belonged to the Lord of Darkness, Ta'aroa. If this was not broken, no revival would last long, And 'Io would never again be the Lord over Hawai'i. The human sacrifice luakini heiau(s)—like the suckers of Ta'aroa's tentacles—remained attached to the land by the blood of their human sacrifices. This was a huge key!

Daniel also found an interesting connection between Tahiti and the luakini heiau(s) in Hawai'i. He found that Pā'ao brought "Mana Stones" (stones containing spiritual power) from his temple, Taputapuatea, to Hawai'i to "plant seeds" or "eggs" of Ta'aroa and 'Oro in Hawai'i. Hawaiian historian Rudy Mitchell wrote that *"Nearly every marae (heiau) of the Society Islands (Tahiti) was an offshoot of some earlier one forming a continuity which was substantiated in the founding stone.[1] This stone, which was sacred, was obtained from the original marae...then it was placed in the new marae, thus starting a new family line and dynasty away from the original."* These stones were "planted" by Pā'ao in the first human sacrifice heiau in Hawai'i at Waha'ula, thus establishing a tentacle of Ta'aroa from Tahiti in Hawai'i.

When demonic *mana* was built up within a heiau through human sacrifice, sacred mana seed stones were taken to build another. The kahuna(s) would pray and ask "the gods" where to plant the next heiau. Daniel found that the seed stones taken to build the new heiau(s) were lined up in rows like the tentacles of Ta'aroa spreading over the islands. They criss-crossed the mountains, valleys and seas of the Hawaiian Islands like a giant web. Daniel collected all of this information thinking he would turn it over to someone who worked in Strategic Prayer. Daniel himself hated Strategic Prayer. He knew firsthand the high cost of coming directly against spiritual principalities and powers. To come against a prince of the magnitude of Ta'aroa would be sheer madness unless God was directing it. Daniel had learned many valuable lessons in his "battles" with spiritual forces, none of which he would like to repeat. The main lesson he learned: without Jesus, he had no power. Daniel would not move into this area unless he received a direct order from God and the Lord had not called him into this area of ministry. He would find someone whose love and calling was Strategic Prayer to hand this information off to. Daniel was glad this was not his ministry. He didn't want to touch this project with a ten-foot pole!

# 13

# Will You Do This For Me?

*"But Jesus beheld them, and said unto them, 'With men this is impossible; but with God all things are possible."*

—Matthew 19:26 KJV

In early 1996, Daniel was awakened one morning by the Lord's presence in the room. Daniel began thanking God for all He had done for him. Then he asked of God his usual prayer. *"Lord, I love you, what can I do for you? I just want to do something for you so I can express my love and gratitude to you."* Suddenly, the Lord spoke. This wasn't just a feeling in his gut, his na'au, that God wanted him to do something. This was one of those rare occasions when Daniel clearly heard His voice.

The Lord first "downloaded" to Daniel in an instant what He desired to be done. Ta'aroa's tentacles of bondage over the islands needed to be removed for God's plan in Hawai'i to reach the next step. The tentacles must be removed all at once. If not, it would be like trying to pull the suckers of a giant octopus off one by one. You would remove one and while working on removing the next, the first one would suction back down. The tentacles of the octopus needed to be removed all at one time. However, if one tried to yank the tentacles of a giant octopus off of someone's arm without first disabling the suckers, it would rip the flesh right off. God would not do that to His beloved Hawai'i. He needed to disable the suction cups of the tentacles first.

The claim Ta'aroa had to suction himself to the land was the innocent blood of men spilled in sacrifice to him. The suction cups of his tentacles were the luakini heiau(s). If Hawaiians repented of this sin, God would forgive (2 Chronicles 7:14), and then Ta'aroa would have no more claim to the land!

Most Christians repent of their own sins and never think of standing before God for the sins of their people groups, nations, cities or regions (Ezek. 22:30, Daniel 9, Ezra 9, Nehemiah 9). Therefore, the healing of the land and the breaking of the curses over peoples, nations, cities and regions almost never happens (Deut. 28). Consequently, revival can take place in individual hearts but not have a lasting effect on the people group, nation or land. Until the stewards of the land stand in repentance for the sins on the land, the curse will remain (Deut. 21:1-9). The spiritual Prince, to whom stewardship of the land was turned over through worship, has the right to remain as Lord of the Land. Most revivals last less than 10 years because they take place in the hearts of men but the spiritual Prince remains as Lord of the Land, eventually re-asserting his control. The revival in Hawai'i was great but Ta'aroa remained as Lord, twisting his tentacles into it. The revival waned within 10 years.

In the Bible, King David broke the curse of a famine on the land of Israel, caused by the breaking of a covenant made in God's name and the shedding of innocent blood (2 Sam. 21:1-14). He did this by fulfilling the law that cleanses this sin which required the death of the murderer (Numbers 35:33). Thank God we no longer need to kill people or even an animal to cleanse the land of sin; Jesus died for our sins once and for all. However, we still need to apply His gift to cleanse the land the same way we need to apply it to cleanse our own lives. It is Jesus who does it all.

Yes, the people living in Hawai'i today had not sacrificed any humans to Ta'aroa and it was not their sin. However, the curse of the innocent blood still remained on the land. As the current spiritual stewards of the land, they are given the responsibility and the authority to cleanse the land of sin (Deut. 21:1-9). They needed to stand before the Lord for the sins of their ancestors as the biblical Daniel did.

Daniel and the people of Israel of his time were captives in Babylon as a result of a Biblical curse caused by the sins of their ancestors. In 538 BC, Daniel read the prophecy of Jeremiah (Jer. 25:11-12) and understood that it was time for his people to be released from the curse of captivity. The Spirit of God convicted Daniel to repent for the sins of his forefathers and his people. As Jesus did, he identified with sins he did not commit and pleaded for God to forgive them. In the remarkable prayer in Daniel 9, he associates himself with the sins of his forefathers and his people 32 times! He does not rail against the "evil" Babylonians who took them into captivity, poked out the eyes of their kings, castrated their men and committed many other horrors upon them. He does not ask God to curse the Babylonians for tormenting his people or to force them to release Israel. Instead he humbly admits to the sins of his <u>own</u> people, taking responsibility for the evils that have befallen them because of their sins. In Daniel 9:11a, Daniel prays, "*Yea, all Israel have transgressed thy law, even by departing that they might not obey thy voice; therefore the curse is poured upon us...*" He then falls upon the mercy of God praying, "*O my God incline thine ear, and hear; open thine eyes, and behold our desolations...for we do not present our supplications before thee for our righteousness, but for thy great mercies*" (Daniel 9:18 KJV).

God was not sitting in heaven waiting for them to commit a sin so He could punish them. He was letting them know that if they polluted and defiled the 'āina (land) with sin, He could not protect them from the evil results unless they repented of their sins. God heard Daniel's humble cry and answered his prayer. That very year King Cyrus fulfilled the prophecy by issuing a decree that the Israelites could return home! Knowing God's will, humility and repentance are the true "Spiritual Warfare!"

If the current people of Hawai'i repented for the sins of their ancestors as Daniel did, God said He would forgive. The power of Ta'aroa, the pollution and defilement of the land by innocent blood, would be removed. His right to claim the land broken, he would have to release it. If this release happened all at once, the tentacles of Ta'aroa would simply fall away from Hawai'i. They would have no place to stick onto the land.

Then the Lord asked in an audible voice, like a loving father gently asking his son for a favor, "*Would you do this for me?*" Daniel was touched by the way his Lord asked him to do this, at the same time, he also felt trapped. After praying often, "*God I love you, is there anything I can do for you?*" God had finally answered him. How could he say no? So many questions fluttered rapidly through Daniel's mind. "*Why me, Lord? Who am I? Shouldn't a person of Hawaiian ancestry lead this mission? It doesn't seem right for me to lead it!*"

Daniel was also very hesitant for another reason. He dreaded with all his being taking this on. He hated "Spiritual Warfare." To spiritually break the power of a network of over a hundred human sacrifice heiau(s) across the islands where many thousands of people were murdered was coming against the tap root, stronghold of the most formidable spiritual power in Hawai'i.

Daniel knew many people in a church that had researched and identified one demonic stronghold over a certain valley in Honolulu and had prayed directly against it. Over the next several years, they told him how members of their church and their families were torn apart by unusual diseases and problems; strange people came into the church causing division; there were demonic presences that attacked in the night; there was adultery, divorce, fights and division between church members; the pastor fell into adultery; and the church closed down.

A very real war raged in spiritual realms. Yet through it all, God had strengthened the survivors. They had gained much experience in identifying the attacks of the enemy and how to protect themselves with the armor of God. Yes, the greater the opposition one faces, the greater the wisdom and strength one gains, but it was so extremely painful and heartrending! Daniel had similar experiences, and they were so painful he did not even want to think about them. Over the years, he had learned about many other people who had prayed directly against demonic principalities and suffered similar devastating consequences. Daniel knew clearly this was no game, and there was no way he wanted to experience something like that again. He had to do it God's way this time!

To say that Daniel really did not want to do it would be the understatement of the century! This project could end up taking many years of grueling and complicated work. But more than that, it would surely entail the dogged attacks of the enemy every step of the way, resulting in perhaps years of pain and heartaches. By this time, in early 1996, the ministry of *Aloha Ke Akua* had expanded to include other native people groups. Not only did Daniel love helping set indigenous people free, but there was still so much work to be done in Hawai'i. It was a detour from his mission that could take the rest of his life to accomplish! He couldn't imagine how he could gather and hold together an organization of people across the islands long enough to complete this task. One of the main tactics of the enemy was division! How could he pull this project off? He would need hundreds of people working in unity across six major islands! In other words, it was impossible for man to do. Daniel knew he couldn't pull it off, but he knew that God could!

Daniel, however, could not say "No" to his Lord. *"Yes, I will do it for you, Lord. Show me the others You have prepared for such a time as this. You are the only One who can do it. It is Your plan and Your work and when it succeeds, only You will get the glory!"*

# 14
# God's Simple Plan

*"O the princely son, first born of divine power!*
*O the Lord of everything, here, there, and always.*
*O the Lord of the heavens and the entire sky.*
*O the princely son, first born of the exalted power.*
*O the son, equal with the father and with Ono (the spirit).*
*Dwelling in the same place.*
*Joined are they three in the same power.*
*The Father, Ono, and the Son."*

—An ancient Marquesan chant

Daniel's wife, Landa, hated to get involved in this kind of project more than Daniel did, but he would never take on such a task if he and his wife were not in unity about it. Daniel was truly shocked when Landa immediately confirmed that he needed to do it. This had to be of God! What a relief to have his closest confidant and advisor supporting him.

He next went to Kawika and Leon who both confirmed that he should do it. Kawika and Leon would continue their work of setting indigenous people free of the three cords; he would work on his task from God.

Daniel prayed, seeking God for His plan of action. He knew, to accomplish this daunting task, it would take the plan of an omnipotent, omniscient God and not his own! Besides, if Jesus said, *"Truly, truly, I say to you, the Son can do nothing of Himself, unless it is something He sees the Father doing; for whatever the Father does, these things the Son also does in like manner"* (John 5:19 NAS), who was Daniel to think he could do this on his own?

Daniel was thinking that for such a huge project, there must be an elaborate secret plan. However, God's ways are not our ways. Like the Good News, the simple story of Jesus sacrificing Himself for us in His love, men want to complicate it with their human pride. God's plan was simple.

The plan was in a simple Scripture, 2 Chronicles 7:14 (NKJV), *"If my people, who are called by my name, will humble themselves, and pray, and seek my face, and turn from their wicked ways; then will I hear from heaven, and will forgive their sin, and will heal their land."* How simple it was! No one could take pride in what they did. They would simply go out to all of the human sacrifice heiau and repent for the sins of their forefathers and their people. God would cleanse and heal the 'āina simply because He loved His children and wanted to restore their land!

God had already called those He wanted to be a part of this mission. He would speak to their hearts. God would do it all. Daniel needed only to walk out His simple plan. He could not fail because he would be following the instructions of the omnipotent God who would do the work! It was the omnipotent God who would defeat the malevolent Lord of Polynesia over Hawai'i. The only thing Daniel felt in his *na'au* they should do was repent, have communion in remembrance of what Jesus had sacrificed to cleanse their sins, and then pour the communion wine and plant the bread into the ground to represent that Jesus also cleanses the land of the curse of sin.

Because *Aloha Ke Akua* had helped Hawaiians and churches of many denominations on every Hawaiian Island, and because of his book, *Perpetuated In Righteousness*, Daniel had more contacts across the islands than most people did. Still, he knew there would be years of spiritual warfare, intense prayer, research to find all of the heiau(s), recruiting and organizing the many teams necessary on each island, and many other components to walking out God's plan; but if they remained in faith and were right in their spirits, Daniel knew they would succeed.

———

In the summer of 1996, Aloha Ke Akua led a short-term friendship mission of Hawaiian musicians and hula dancers to two First Nations' (Native American) reservations, one in Victoria on Vancouver Island and the other in Prince George, B.C., Canada. They also participated in a conference in Victoria where an acquaintance of Daniel was in charge of the prayer covering. This man was one of the most respected and experienced in the area of strategic prayer, and Daniel had asked him for his advice on the project God had placed in his hands. They met one evening and Daniel was given much good advice for the project. But before they parted, this man had something he needed to tell Daniel. He said, *"I had been speaking in Hawai'i when a friend of mine asked me to pray over a human sacrifice heiau on the property of a ministry she was helping to develop. I went with her to the property and we walked the heiau and prayed over it. When I returned home, I became so ill that I nearly died, I am still recovering from it. While I was ill in bed, I asked the Lord why this illness had come upon me. God answered and said, 'Because I did not tell you* to go to the heiau and pray. You were not under my covering. Praying over the heiau(s) in Hawai'i is not for you to do; it is for the Hawaiian people to do.' I am telling you now that you are the ones that God has anointed to cleanse the heiau(s). You are on the right track, go for it!"

# 15
# Key People Emerge

*'A'ohe hana i nele i ka uku.*
*No task is too big when done together by all.*
—a Hawaiian saying

Daniel started working 60 to 70 hours a week on God's assignment. He knew he could not stop until his mission was accomplished. *"I decided I would share about this special mission with only those I felt led to contact after much prayer. This assignment was not for the immature Christian or the Christian struggling with sin. It was for the mature, experienced and proven prayer warrior."*

Daniel needed teams on each island but he couldn't go for numbers; he had to go for quality. He realized that the more carefully he picked his "special forces," the fewer attacks and problems there would be for everyone involved. He prayed often over who God wanted to be a part of this mission, especially for the right island and district coordinators. At the same time, he knew he could never "get it all perfect" because he was imperfect! The leaders would need to humbly do their best and give God the rest. He looked for veteran prayer warriors and asked them to hand pick others they knew on their islands.

Another concern was the heiau locations. Daniel had heard rumors of secret *luakini heiau(s)*. The vast majority of *heiau(s)* were well mapped out by the State of Hawai'i, preserved as archeological sites. But what if there were secret ones they did not pray over? Some had also been destroyed by farmers and developers before the State started its archeological protection program, so only knowledge of their general location remained. There might also be *luakini heiau(s)* on the restricted islands of Ni'ihau and Kaho'olawe. What if they could not gain access? Would the 'Io Project fulfill God's plan if they were not able to pray over all of the *luakini heiau(s)*?

As Daniel prayed about this problem, God gave him a vision of a spider's web. A spider's web has several main strands that anchor it in place. God showed Daniel that, if these main strands of the web were taken down, the entire web would fall. They need not find every single one, they were not doing it, God was! He would lead them to the necessary heiau(s) in the main strands. This humbling revelation affirmed that God was using them, and only He could make the plan succeed. There would be glory for no one except their God.

On each island, God called His people to fulfill the task at hand; some came excitedly and some came reluctantly. The common factor: they were all called by God for such a time as this.

*"God told me to approach this mission with great caution and secrecy—like the underground resistance in a land occupied by*

*the enemy," said Daniel. "I held invitation-only meetings on each island telling everyone present to keep the project to themselves. We prayed that God would blind the eyes of Ta'aroa and his minions from seeing what we were doing. Like a Special Forces' team of ants, we quietly went about our plans to take his strength away right under the giant tentacles of Ta'aroa."*

## Maui

Daniel's hanai brother, Akea, still lived on Maui. Through their 22-year friendship Daniel would often call Akea for advice on Hawaiian issues. And because of their trust and common commitment to the Hawaiian people, Akea, naturally, became a leader in the 'Io Project. It was the Maui group that coined the name, the 'Io Project. The Maui coordinator, a descendent of Ali'i(s) named Kaulana Correa, called for regular prayer meetings until the project was done. A handful of committed leaders—Kaulana Correa, Jill and Tia Tahauri, George Kaimiola, Jacob Mau, and Akea—came out of those meetings.

## Moloka'i

### *John Kūpuna*
### *Hālawa Valley*

John Kūpuna grew up roaming the back country of his native Moloka'i. He knew well how to hunt and fish and live off the land. But this bright young man also had a heart for God, and he was chosen by his father to be the kahu (pastor)

of their family church. For years his father had been training him for this purpose. One day, as they spoke of spiritual
things, John's father revealed their family's darkest secret.
With great sadness and remorse he told John that his great,
great grandfather and grandmother were kahuna 'anā'anā.
They had eaten the first-born sons of each generation in the
hidden tradition of kahuna 'anā'anā. John was shocked. He
questioned how he could be descended from such people and
how this stain could ever be removed from their family.

Soon after he became kahu, John went out hunting one
day with his cousin. Young and strong, John was in his element as he hiked Hālawa Valley searching for deer and goat.
It was on this day that he came across a heiau hidden in the
brush. Suddenly, he had a vision of blood, blood everywhere,
blood all across the heiau, blood dripping and oozing down the
heiau. The blood of his people who were sacrificed here. His
spirit responded in horror and revulsion at the shedding of so
much innocent blood and he began to weep uncontrollably.

"John! John!" he heard his cousin calling his name and
quickly composed himself. *"Bra, wait, I stay coming!"* he said
as he walked towards his cousin wiping his eyes. *"Wow, what
was that all about!"* he had thought.

Now, years later, John was sitting in a meeting. Somehow,
he had been invited to hear Daniel Kikawa speak about some
secret Hawaiian project. *"I was very skeptical. I thought, 'What
can dis Japanese guy tell me about Hawaiian stuff and Moloka'i?
I am Hawaiian and I grew up here.'"* At the same time John felt
humbled in the presence of the older pastors from Moloka'i
who were in the meeting. When Daniel started talking about
the innocent blood, the curse on the land, 2 Chronicles 7:14
and about the healing of the land. John knew it was the truth
and his spirit rose up inside of him. He thought back to the
supernatural grief he experienced after seeing the vision of

blood covering the heiau he'd discovered while hunting several years before. He knew immediately God had destined him to be a part of this project. He had to go and cleanse the family lands of Hālawa Valley. He committed right there to be overseer of the Hālawa team.

———

## Kauaʻi

### Kehilat O Ka Mesia

Ben and Lydia were Jewish believers in Yeshua (Jesus) and had a congregation on the island of Kauaʻi called, "Kehilat O Ka Mesia." *Kehilat* is Hebrew for congregation and *O Ka Mesia*, Hawaiian for the Messiah. It was a good description of what their congregation was like, a combination of Hawaiian and Jewish styles. Their elders were Iokepa and Kepola. Kepola was from a well known Hawaiian hula family on Kauaʻi and a descendant of aliʻi(s), kahu(s), music composers, and historians.

Kepola was a long-time friend of Leon Siu, one of the three founders of Aloha Ke Akua. Daniel met her and Iokepa when she danced the hula at the first event Aloha Ke Akua held on Kauaʻi. Since then, they also had become good friends. Whenever Aloha Ke Akua held an event or meeting on Kauaʻi, they were front and center to help. Daniel knew he could count on them, and they were the first ones he approached about the ʻIo Project. He met with them at their home and was introduced to Ben at that time. When Daniel shared about the ʻIo Project, they all affirmed the importance of the mission and committed to the project without hesitation.

———

# Oʻahu

## *Kahu Dean Spencer*
## *Papakōlea*

Kahu Dean Spencer was a Hawaiian man with a heart for his Hawaiian homestead of Papakōlea at the base of Punchbowl Crater. He had heard about the human sacrifices at Punchbowl and that kapu breakers were drowned at Kewalo basin, directly to the sea from Punchbowl. When Daniel told him about the ʻIo Project, he knew God was calling him to be involved, specifically to cleanse areas connected to his beloved homestead. But Dean was reluctant to commit. He and his wife Robin had suffered a terrible price for their confrontations with sinister spiritual forces in the past. He couldn't imagine trying to take on such a powerful spiritual lord over their area.

Having grown up in Papakōlea, Dean had seen first-hand the power of the spiritual forces residing there. There was a trail where night marchers (a procession of Hawaiian spirits) walked near his home. He had seen an akualele there (a comet-like spiritual fireball believed sent by kahuna ʻanāʻanā to destroy someone). Many believed that if you got in the way of an akualele, it would chase after you instead! Another friend had a son who was driving across the trail of the Night Marchers one night. His car suddenly died right on their path for no reason and he was pinned down to his seat by invisible powers. When he got home into the light, they discovered that he was covered with scratch marks all over his body. A kūpuna had told him that the bodies of people killed in Kewalo Basin were carried up to Punchbowl via that trail.

Dean had struggled to pastor people living in fear of these spirits. He was so burned out from waging spiritual warfare that he didn't even want to think of the cost of taking on such a project. Though he knew God was telling him to do this, Dean was, as locals called it, "*making deaf ear*" to God about it. Daniel wasn't worried though. He knew Dean and Robin would always obey God. In the end, Dean reluctantly agreed to be responsible for the Punchbowl to Kewalo area.

---

## Big Island

### Beth Naholowaʻa Murph

Beth Naholowaʻa Murph came from a prominent Hawaiian family but had lived most of her life on the Mainland. She had met and married her husband, Tim, who was part-Cherokee, while living there. However, in 1990, God told them to move back to Hawaiʻi. They obeyed, not knowing why, only that God was going to do <u>something</u> in Hawaiʻi, and He wanted them to play a role in it. The Lord moved them to the Hilo area, where they served the Lord as He directed them. But Tim and Beth knew that they had not yet accomplished that for which God had called them to Hawaiʻi. In the fall of 1995 Beth fasted and prayed for 40 days. Her cry was, "*What did you call us to Hawaiʻi for, Lord? What is the mission you had us move all the way from California for?*"

Two years later, Daniel was asking different pastors and intercessors for names of people they thought should be involved in the ʻIo Project. The name Beth Naholowaʻa Murph came up several times. Daniel finally tracked her down and found that the Murphs lived near his home. He asked Beth and Tim if they would be involved with the ʻIo Project. They said they needed to ask the Lord first. They were experienced in spiritual warfare and knew better than to get involved unless God told them to. This was just the kind of people Daniel was looking for. He was sure God would tell them to be involved.

After a few weeks of prayer, the Murphs said they were ready to be involved. Because they lived near each other, Beth and Tim, and Daniel and Landa soon were praying and planning the 'Io Project together.

In the fall of 1997, Beth went to a prayer conference on Kaua'i. She loved praying and God spoke to her often in prayer. On the second day of the conference Beth was preparing to go to the morning prayer meeting when she heard the Lord's voice once again.

*"Don't go to the prayer meeting, stay and spend time alone with me."*

*"Yes, Lord,"* she replied.

Beth immediately sat down to wait upon the Lord. The Lord spoke a second time saying, *"The hem of my garment will soon pass over Hawai'i."* Then suddenly a vision passed before her eyes. She saw the giant hem of the Lord's garment passing over the islands. It was so huge it swept over whole islands at a time. Then she saw golden pearls rolling down the Lord's garment and off of the hem. When these pearls hit the islands, they burst into golden liquid that flowed over the land. That is when she realized these golden pearls were spheres of oil. It was the Lord's anointing falling upon the Islands of Hawai'i! Beth looked on in excitement: there were thousands of golden pearls flowing off of God's garment onto the islands! Each place a pearl dropped, she knew the anointing of the Lord would fall upon different ones and they would do special things for Him.

Then the Lord spoke one last time, *"You are to go to the top of Mauna Kea and pray for the Hawaiian Islands,"* and then, there was silence. As suddenly as the Lord's voice had come, it was gone.

Now everything became clear to Beth. She finally knew why she was called home to her beloved Hawai'i. It was for the 'Io Project! And now she finally had her instructions from God on her place in it. Although it was not a place of human sacrifice, she was to go to the top of Mauna Kea, the highest point in the islands, and pray for Hawai'i. Finally, the time had come! They were called to Hawai'i for such a time as this!

## Kahu John Trusdell

Kahu John Trusdell became close friends with Daniel Kikawa after he moved to Hilo. When Daniel told John about the 'Io Project, John responded with a surprising revelation. Kahu John was a descendant of Hewahewa, the last kahuna nui (high priest) of the Kapu System. He was, therefore, a descendant of Pā'ao. Kahu John chose to be responsible for cleansing the first human sacrifice heiau that Pā'ao had established in Hawai'i, the imposing Waha'ula heiau. It sat directly below Kīlauea, one of the most active volcanoes in the world.

Over the many centuries since Pā'ao had arrived and established Waha'ula, the lava flowing down Kīlauea to the ocean never came near the heiau. In June of 1989, one lava flow overran and destroyed the National Park Visitor Center next to Waha'ula heiau but did not touch Waha'ula. One of the flows of molten lava rock burned its way went right up to the walls of Waha'ula and then went right around it to the ocean. There Waha'ula remained, defiant, in the middle of barren lava fields that had covered the road, the visitor center, and everything else for many miles around. God chose a man He could rely on for this daunting assignment.

### Pastor Alan Cravalho
### Honoka'a

Alan Cravalho, the pastor of King's Chapel Honoka'a on the Big Island, can seem intimidating at first meeting. Though not particularly tall, he's a big man (about 240 pounds) with a "wide body" and an electrifying spiritual intensity. Pastor Alan also happens to be a really nice guy and funny, too. God called him to the Big Island to start an extension of King's Cathedral, the largest church on Maui. Alan's senior pastor, Dr. James Marocco, knew he was the right man for this difficult job because he knew Alan's nature. He was a great prayer warrior, and he was not a quitter. To Daniel, Alan seemed like a clone of Dr. Marocco both physically and spiritually. Daniel knew it would take a pastor with unusual determination and grit to pray through and firmly plant a church in the old sugar plantation town of Honoka'a. And Alan Cravalho was just such a man.

Pastor Alan's church, King's Chapel Honoka'a, followed the example of King's Cathedral Maui by holding prayer meetings six days a week from 5:30a.m.—6:30 a.m. Pastor Alan could be found praying at that time Sunday mornings too. He also fasted often. Fasts of 21 days on water and 40 days on juices were not uncommon for him! But Pastor Alan loved it; he said it was when he heard the Lord speak the clearest.

One day while in prayer, God told Pastor Alan that he was to be, *"the Gate Keeper to the valleys."* Not being sure what this meant, Pastor Alan had begun to research the valleys of the area even before he heard of the 'Io Project. He knew that Waipi'o Valley was spiritually significant. However, after his research, he was convinced that nearby Waimanu Valley was the hidden key to the release of the North Kohala and Hāmākua areas of the Big Island for the purposes of God.

When he heard about the 'Io Project several months later he said, "*I know this is of God! He has been preparing me for this already, and I know exactly where I need to go, Waimanu Valley!*" Because of the area's spiritual significance, Alan knew he would be facing a powerful spiritual ruler. He knew also that if it was a critical key to the North Kohala and Hāmākua areas, it was also a critical key for the success of the whole 'Io Project. Pastor Alan had plenty of experience in warfare with the forces of darkness. God had told him that his church was to be a warrior church that was not afraid of battle. Pastor Alan set his jaw and immediately began praying fervently for the 'Io Project.

## Island Breeze
## Kona

Island Breeze is a missionary organization born out of Youth With A Mission (YWAM). In 1985, Island Breeze began using Polynesian dances to worship God. At this time, most church leaders thought Polynesian dances were pagan and should not be used in Christian worship. Island Breeze believed this aspect of their culture could be redeemed and went through many trials as they followed what God told them to do. They became the spearhead of the indigenous Christian movement, and Daniel considered them his elders. Island Breeze and Aloha Ke Akua became closely linked ministries. Island Breeze eventually became an international movement with branches not only throughout Polynesia but in Africa, Asia, and North and South America.

To support their missionary work, West Hawai'i's Island Breeze group began a secular business doing lū'au shows. For many years they have been ranked as the top lū'au show on the Big Island. Their show is held at the King Kamehameha Hotel, right on the beach in the resort town of Kailua-Kona.

The hotel is called the King Kamehameha because it sits on the lands where the king used to live.

Also on the grounds of the hotel is the restored Ahuʻena heiau. This heiau was said to have been built in the 15th century and used for human sacrifices. It was rebuilt by Kamehameha as the official state heiau in the early 1800s. The king dedicated it to Lono, the Hawaiian god of peace, possibly because he had unified the islands and peace is what the new Hawaiian government desired. No human sacrifices were made there after this time.

Ahuʻena heiau sits on a peninsula of land that curves around a small sandy bay in front of the King Kamehameha Hotel. This bay is called Kamakahonu, "The Eye of the Turtle," and is one of the most sacred sites in Kona. It was here that Kamehameha moved his seat of government in 1812. It was also here, just six months after his death in 1819, that his son and heir, Liholiho (King Kamehameha II), Kamehameha's sacred wife, Queen Keʻopuolani and his favorite wife Queen Kaʻahumanu broke the ancient Kapu System by sharing a meal together. Because men and women were not allowed to eat together under the Kapu System, the breaking of this most visible kapu by the highest aliʻi(s) in the land spelled the end of the old religious system. Some say the first heiau torched by Hewahewa, the last high priest of the Kapu System and a direct descendant of Pāʻao, was Ahuʻena.

Island Breeze's lūʻau show was held near the former Ahuʻena heiau grounds. They naturally committed to pray for this *heiau*, not only because their lūʻau was held there, but because the *kumu hula* (hula master) of Island Breeze, Paoakalani, was a Kamehameha family descendant. Daniel had no worries about this heiau; he knew Island Breeze would pray and do whatever God told them.

## Pastor "Tex" Texeira
## West Hawai'i

At a private meeting in Kona in early 1997, Daniel shared about the 'Io Project with a select group of Christian leaders that included Pastor James "Tex" Texeira of Solid Rock Ministries. Pastor Tex listened intently as Daniel spoke the Word of the Lord:

*"Behold, the* LORD's *hand is not so short that it cannot save; Nor is His ear so dull that it cannot hear. But your iniquities have made a separation between you and your God, And your sins have hidden His face from you so that He does not hear"* (Isaiah 59:1-2 NAS).

*"It is difficult to look at our own sins but it is OUR sins that separate us from God. If we make right with God, He has promised to heal our land."*

Daniel then read from 2 Chronicles 7:13-15 (KJV), *"If I shut up heaven that there be no rain, or if I command the locusts to devour the land, or if I send pestilence among my people; If my people, which are called by my name, shall humble themselves, and pray, and seek my face, and turn from their wicked ways; then will I hear from heaven, and will forgive their sin, and will heal their land. Now mine eyes shall be open, and mine ears attend unto the prayer that is made in this place."*

Daniel then spoke words that cut to Pastor Tex's heart: *"If there is any warfare, it is with our own pride which keeps us from seeing our sins, humbling ourselves before God, and repenting. If there is anything we need to do, it is to make sure we are right with God, our fellow man and have been a proper kahu (steward) over the 'āina He has given to us; and that we are following God's instructions to be a part of this project. If not, you are not protected from the Prince of Darkness and the cost may be severe to you and possibly your whole team. This is not a game! Count the cost before committing to this project. Make sure you hear from God to be a part of this project. He loves you and knows what is best for you. There is no way I would be doing this if God did not ask me to. Even Jesus said he could do nothing of himself but could only do what he first saw his Father in Heaven doing. Who are we to think we can do this on our own if even Jesus could not? If we do, it is pride and sin, and we will not be under God's protection."*

When Daniel sat down, "Pastor Tex" stood up to talk.

*"I had been one of the pastors of a church on Maui. It was a growing vital church with five ministers. One day, a witch came to know the love of Jesus. She told us about a 'power place' where the witches went to pray. We five pastors decided this was a place of the devil and that it should be destroyed to set people free. We went out to the place to 'stomp on the devil.' We were the mighty people of God and we were going to chase the devil out. When we got to the place, we yelled at the devil to leave, stomped on the ground and kicked the dirt, but God did not tell us to do this.*

*One by one, Satan took us down. One minister died, two got divorced, and one left the church to go to a cult. Only I was left, and I was very ill. I went to doctor after doctor to find out what was wrong. None of the doctors could figure out what was wrong with me, but they all agreed that I was dying. It wasn't until a prophet came to my church and told me, 'I see the spirit of death over you,' and prayed for me, that I got well. I know the cost per-sonally,"* Tex said, *"but I will be a part of this project because I know it is right and it is being done in the right way."*

Daniel admired his guts; here was a man who would do what Jesus told him even after what he experienced. Tex was one who had learned the same lesson Daniel had: we are nothing without Jesus! He was just the kind of spiritual war-rior who would survive.

In closing, Daniel told the leaders, *"As far as I know, in no geographical area on the magnitude of a state has there been attempted such a comprehensive project as to completely take down the root stronghold of the Prince of that land. I believe that it is because the first shall be last and the last shall be first. Geographically, Hawai'i is not only the farthest place from Israel but, as far as I know, it is also the last area on earth to be inhabited. Archeologists estimate the time of the first arrival of man in the Hawaiian Islands at somewhere around 400 AD. These islands are, spiritually, the cleanest on earth! Man was killing innocent man for at least 6000 years in the Middle East. Human sacrifice was rampant by 4000 BC. By contrast, the first human sacrifice in Hawai'i wasn't until around 1200 AD! By cleansing this tap root sin of human sacrifice, the islands can be cleansed and returned to 'Io. Could this be the time for the last to be first? Let's pray."*

God worked on the hearts of His people and they began to come forward to be responsible for heiau(s) in the areas that the Lord showed to them. It was all God's doing.

### Moke

As Daniel was asking different Hawaiian Christians if they would join in this project, he naturally asked Moke if he would be a part of it. Moke agreed that this must be done and said he wanted to go to his family heiau on the northern side of the Big Island. He had never been to this out-of-the-way place, but he had heard it was a human sacrifice heiau. Daniel agreed there would be no better person to go to that heiau and repent than a descendant of the kahuna(s) of that heiau.

Thus, the journey began, everyone working to fulfill God's plan step by step...no one having a clue about God's hidden agenda and His full purpose for the 'Io Project.

# 16
# Preparations

*"Yea, though I walk through the valley of the shadow of death,
I will fear no evil: for thou art with me…"*

—Psalm 23:4a KJV

## Moloka'i

*John Kūpuna*
*Hālawa Valley*

John Kūpuna woke violently, gasping for breath and dripping in cold sweat. He had the same terrifying dream again. And yet, it was more than a dream, it was real. It seemed as if his soul had been wrenched from his body and thrown into some shadowy realm of horror. The dream was becoming more and more frequent as the time of the 'Io Project approached. It was always the same. He was smothered by powerful invisible forces, bound by cords and abducted to a high place where he was whipped and beaten by shadowy apparitions. It was so real that his soul seemed to ache when he awoke. It seemed they were trying desperately to kill him. Powerful invisible hands would grip his mouth, smothering him, preventing him from speaking, but at the last moment, just before they would kill him, he always managed to call upon Jesus. He would struggle and struggle and finally, with all of his might, just be able to mumble that precious name above all names. As he spoke that name over and over, louder and louder, he would suddenly awaken, the name of Jesus on his lips.

John knew this was an attack by the vicious spirits that his ancestors, the kahuna ʻanāʻanā, had served. They were in a desperate struggle to stop him from breaking their grip upon his family and the land. As long as the blood was not cleansed, these evil spirits still held power over them. But John was a warrior and this only made him more determined. His faith in God made him fearless. John spoke out loud, "*To live or die is gain in Christ!*"

---

## Big Island

### *Kahu John Trusdell*

On August 12, 1997, during preparations for the ʻIo project, after nearly 800 years, a lava flow from Kīlauea finally overran and destroyed Wahaʻula heiau. Kahu John Trusdell's ʻIo project team looked at this as a sign of spiritual cleansing to come, the first luakini heiau, cleansed sovereignly by the fire of God.

## Ka'u

The team from Solid Rock Ministries, Pastor Tex's church in Kona, was assigned three heiau(s) in Ka'u. Several weeks before the 'Io Project, they were having difficulty finding the sites. They stopped at the little town of Waiohinu to get something to drink. A kūpuna was sitting there at the store and noticed them studying the map. She was a tough old rancher and a little intimidating. *"What you looking for?"* she asked gruffly. They told her they were looking for three heiau(s). The kūpuna replied, *"I am from Ka'u and for many years I had felt this urge to find out where all of the heiau(s) in Ka'u were, I don't know why. I know exactly where they are. Come, I will show you."* The team couldn't believe the provision and favor of God. God had been putting this burden on the kūpuna to find the heiau(s) in Ka'u for such a time as this! She led them to two of the heiau(s) but the third was behind several locked gates on a ranch. Fortunately, it was on her cousin's ranch! She could not reach him by phone but said she would meet the Solid Rock team at the gate on March 14th to let them in and then she left. They were just sitting at the gate when the rancher drove down. *"What are you looking for?"* he asked. They told him about the heiau and why they wanted to go there. He said, *"Sure. I will take you there. Weird things happen there, I would love to have you pray over it."* The team was stunned by how God in his omnipotence had set everything in place before the 'Io Project was even conceived! All they could say was, *"God is good!"*

## Kona

The team assigned to a key heiau in Kona couldn't find it for a while because it had been completely destroyed. However, through much research they pinpointed the area upon which the heiau had existed. It was in a parking lot in Kona. The next day, an article in the *West Hawaii Today* newspaper identified the parking lot as the town's worst area for drug dealing! There was a curse upon the bloody land even though the heiau was destroyed. The land would soon be cleansed and the curse broken!

### Pastor Alan
### Honoka'a

Pastor Alan never told John and Nalani Subiono, the North Hawai'i Island Coordinators, that he felt he had to go to the heiau(s) in the remote Waimanu Valley. He was a man of prayer and for something as treacherous as this, both spiritually and physically, he was going to make sure God was telling him to go. He kept looking at how inaccessible Waimanu was and kept saying to God, *"Fly in? We are going to fly in aren't we, Lord?"*

The Lord gave him a scripture in prayer, 2 Chronicles 20 (NASB), especially verse 15, *"...thus says the LORD to you, 'Do not fear or be dismayed because of this great multitude, for the battle is not yours but God's."* He knew then he had to go into Waimanu Valley. Pastor Alan knew the Lord had a great battle ahead of him but God would be with him. He also knew Waimanu Valley was a spiritual gateway for the North Kohala area. Most people knew that Waipi'o Valley was a place of great spiritual power but it was nearby Waimanu Valley that was the well-kept secret of Ta'aroa and the real seat of power. It was a key area for the success of the whole 'Io Project. In Pastor Alan, God picked the right man for the job.

Pastor Alan knew he had to have his worship leader with him. So he told his new worship leader, a Hawaiian man named George Ruiz, *"We are going."* George had no choice. George's wife, Tammy, offered to go with them to make up the suggested team of at least three people. Tammy was a prayer warrior and was excited to go on their helicopter mission. All three began to prepare spiritually. George would say later, *"There are times that God withholds the fullness of a picture for our benefit. If we knew what we were getting into, we would not have done it because of fear. This was one of those times."* Little did they know God was about to turn all of their plans upside-down. George, Tammy, and Pastor Alan continued preparations unaware of what they were about to face.

---

## Maui

### *Kahu Mau*
### *Hāna*

Kahu Mau knew this "project" was no game. He was from a well-known and respected Hawaiian family on Maui. He had experienced firsthand the "dark side" of Hawaiian spirituality. Stories abounded in the Hawaiian Islands about people having terrifying encounters with these powerful spiritual forces. Most everyone who had grown up in the Hawaiian community had experienced it or knew someone who had. Hawaiians looked at Westerners who had no fear of these things as naive. Kahu Mau had seen the akualele (flying spirit fireballs), He also knew in his spirit that the 'Io Project had to be done. Kahu Mau was given the assignment of Hāna's luakini heiau, the largest heiau on Maui. He thought to himself, *"The Lord really has a sense of humor sending the smallest church involved in this project to the largest heiau!"* And yet, God's ways are far above our ways! Who would have sent a skinny little boy named David against Goliath! One thing for sure, God created a situation for him where pride was absolutely obliterated! If they were to do this thing, it would be purely the power of God. Kahu Mau approached his task with utter humility and reliance on God. Zechariah 4:6 was his watchword, "*Not by might, nor by power but by my Spirit says the Lord of Hosts.*"

Kahu Mau's first task was to see the caretaker/guardian of the heiau and humbly ask for permission to do what 'Io told them to do. He explained their plan to the man, assuring him the heiau would be treated with utmost respect for his family and not be disturbed in any way physically. The Hawaiian guardian of the heiau not only gave permission but was so touched by what they were going to do there that he prayed with Kahu Mau to accept Iesū. He also agreed to open the gate at 4:30 a.m. Saturday morning.

Kahu Mau's team of five men and seven women spent the week in fervent prayer. On Thursday night, March 12, one of the women dreamed of a man in black running across the grounds of the heiau with a fire chasing after him.

---

## Moloka'i

### John Kūpuna
### Hālawa Valley

John Kūpuna sat listening to his wife's tearful story. She had just heard that the son of one of their friends involved with the 'Io Project had been killed in a freak car accident. There was no way to know if this accident was related to the 'Io Project, but terror filled her face. "*John, I am so afraid about what you are doing. You know all of the stories of people getting ill or dying in weird ways when they mess around with these things. And it is happening now! I have heard of others involved with this project, mostly Hawaiians, who are sick or whose children got hurt. I am so afraid! It is not only for you but what about me and the children? The project is still weeks away and already all these things are happening and what about your recurrent dream! The gods of your family are trying to kill you. What if they succeed? What may happen on that day if all this is happening now!"* John could feel the terror gripping his wife with each spoken fear. The same pervasive, creeping tentacles of fear were beginning to fill the room. He knew that fear and belief in their power increased the control these evil forces had over people. The more people believed in them and feared them, the more power they could wield over them. John's warrior spirit caught flame. He jumped up and began to battle against them for his wife. He knew that if he let the fear in, the dark tentacles would wrap around them and squeeze the faith and hope right out of them. They would then be easy prey for the Lord of Darkness.

*"God did not give us a spirit of fear!"* he proclaimed, *"But of power and of love and a sound mind! We can do all things through Christ who strengthens us! Jesus said, 'I will NEVER leave you or forsake you!'"* All of the scriptures he had learned over the years seemed to come one after another as he warred against the devil with the Word of God. It seemed as if the fire of God was now filling the room, burning out the dark and cold. *"I have the authority because I am doing God's will!"* Dark tentacles slipped away. Then, all was at peace. His wife was at peace. John was doing this project in obedience to God and for his family. He knew he was in for a major battle, but nothing would stop him from setting his family and his children free from these evil spirits that had controlled and tormented his family for generations. Nothing would stop him from cleansing his beloved Hālawa Valley from the sins of his forefathers. He knew that his God was omnipotent and

would keep them safe if they followed his instructions. He would be victorious in Christ!

---

## Worldwide Prayer Shield

God had supernaturally set up divine meetings for Daniel with leaders of prayer organizations from around the world, and God spoke to these leaders to support the "ground troops" in Hawai'i with "air prayer cover" during the 'Io Project. Daniel knew that this "air cover" was vital to the success of the 'Io Project. They would have many thousands of people around the world praying for Hawai'i on that day. It was truly God's project!

---

## The State of Hawai'i

A terrible drought continued on all of the islands and wildfires raged in many places; one even threatened Daniel's home. He believed this was the manifesting of the curses of Deuteronomy 28 upon the land. He also believed that this drought would have to cease when God forgave the sin on the land.

After two years of hard work and many trials, the teams were finally in place. The troops were now ready; they were just waiting for the order from their Captain, Jesus. When did He want the 'Io Project to commence?

# 17
# The Date Revealed

*"Sprang up wars, fierce and long. Atea (Kāne's name in the Marquesan, Atea means light and the first man created in his image was also called Atea. Atea is "Akea" in Hawaiian.) and Tanaoa (Darkness, the Marquesan name for Ta'aroa), great wrath and contention...Tanaoa confined, ...O thrones whereon to seat the Lord of love (Atea); The great Lord Atea established in love...Atea gave nothing back to Tanaoa, Who thus was chased to distant regions, Where the light of day was not known; ...O dark Tanaoa engulfed in the long nights."*

—An ancient Marquesan chant

Leaders of the 'Io Project knew they could not move forward against the spiritual stronghold of the Lord of Darkness, Ta'aroa, without a clear confirmed date from the Lord. When God says to "take an objective," one cannot run out before God gives the order. To do so is to move outside God's authority and protection. In his youthful zeal, Daniel and others had been ravaged by the enemy doing this in the past. They were not going to make the same mistake against the most powerful principality in the islands. They had to be under the orders of their Captain or they were not going to move forward an inch.

Several key intercessors were praying for a confirmed "D-Day" order from the Lord. Daniel asked God to confirm it in a way they could never think up or imagine. That way, they would know it was not fabricated by their own thoughts or wishes.

The Lord had spoken to Beth Naholowa'a Murph in 1997 that, at the time He designated, she was to take her position at the top of Mauna Kea, the tallest mountain in the islands and the tallest in the world if measured from its base on the ocean floor. Mauna Kea was a key high place under the major tentacle of Ta'aroa over the southern islands of Hawai'i which were the Big Island (Hawai'i), Maui and Moloka'i. While in prayer for the date that the 'Io Project was to commence, God told her she was to go to the top of Mauna Kea in the last month of the year and that the key was in the book of Esther.

Then the Lord spoke to Daniel's wife, Landa, that February 27, 1998 was a very important date for this project.

Daniel was confused; one of them must have not heard the Lord. What did December, the last month of the year have to do with February 27, 1998? And yet, he trusted both of them as accurate intercessors.

To add to the confusion, in prayer, Daniel saw the number fourteen rising toward him in blue flames. He rarely saw visions and this one was so clear. Now he was really perplexed! How could December, the last month of the year, February 27 and the number 14 show the date to launch the 'Io Project? Were two of the three people wrong on the timing of God? He decided to research the book of Esther, the only other clue given. The Lord told Beth it held the key.

As Daniel studied the book of Esther, these confusing elements fell into place and everything became crystal clear. All of these dates did fit together! God had confirmed his date in a way they would never think or imagine on their own. They now had their D-Day orders and Daniel sent out the following letter to the district and island coordinators. The 'Io Project had the green light.

## ALOHA KE AKUA

To the Island and District Coordinators,

The date of the 'Io Project is March 14, 1998.

How the date was confirmed. A trusted intercessor was told by the Lord to go to a certain high place. She saw candles going up to this high place and shofar and conches being blown. They danced and sang praises to God, proclaiming that the islands belonged to Him. She was told to go in the last month of the year and that the answers were in Esther. The Lord told my wife that Feb. 27 was a very important date. One day in prayer, I saw a vivid number 14 of blue flame; very unusual for me because I rarely see visions. With this information, which did not seem to fit together at all, I started doing research.

How this all fit together. The story of Esther is primarily about how God saved his people from their enemies. The enemy had planned to wipe out the people of God, but God turned it around and the enemy was wiped out instead. The day that this victory is perpetually celebrated by Israel is called Purim. Purim is held during the *last month* of the Jewish calendar called Adar. This year, the month of Adar begins on our *Feb. 27*. Purim is celebrated on the *14th* day of Adar.

The 14th of Adar actually falls on the 12th of March on our calendar. However, we felt that the number 14 was of the most significance and therefore the project should be held on our calendar 14. The number 14 (double 7) represents God's time of saving grace if we humble ourselves before him and his judgment if we do not. These are times of judgment or grace upon whole nations or peoples, major moves of God.

This is not only seen in Esther but in Math. 1:17 (KJV), "*So all the generations from Abraham to David are fourteen generations; and from David until the carrying away into Babylon are fourteen generations; and from the carrying away into Babylon unto Christ are fourteen generations.*" The fourteenth was also the day that the Passover lamb was slain (Ex. 12:6). It is only because of God's grace and mercy upon us that we escape judgment.

The 14th of March this year also happens to be the Sabbath. Our warfare on this day is the warfare of Daniel 9 and 2nd Chron. 7:14; it is a ceasing from our own works and clinging onto God's mercy and grace towards us. It is a day of fasting, sackcloth and ashes (Dan. 9:3), a day of repentance and humility before God; for only He can forgive our sins and, therefore, deliver us from certain judgment upon our islands. Like Daniel, God asks us to stand in the gap for our land (Ezekiel 22:30). In Daniel 9, Daniel associates himself with the sins of his people 32 times!

The fast of Esther is commemorated on the 13th. I feel that it would be prudent for all of us to fast and pray <u>at least</u> one day. During this time of fasting, we should be looking within our own lives to see if there is any unclean thing in us. Earnestly seek God and ask him to expose any area in our lives that needs cleaning up. We must also be clean with others. Any unforgiveness or bitterness in our lives could be the open door to destroy us and our families. If God tells you to go to someone who has aught against you, GO! God is pinpointing these areas because he loves you and does not want you to get hurt.

Thousands of intercessors from around the world have committed to pray for us. They wait with baited breath for what the Spirit of the Lord will do here.

There may be casualties in this battle, but God knows who is to be in His Gideon's army. We may not find every site, we may not have a person of Hawaiian ancestry in every group, we may not have three or more in each, I believe that this is what God will allow.... to keep us safe from our own pride! No Hawaiian will be able to say we did it. No Intercessor will be able to say we got them all. No one will have glory here except God! The victory will be won purely because He wants to pour out His mercy and grace upon Hawai'i.

As you have probably guessed, I have been praying a lot over this project. The more I pray, the more God convicts me that this is a simple battle, as simple as Jericho. JUST DO WHAT GOD HAS TOLD US TO DO.

*"Have not I commanded thee? Be strong and of good courage; be not afraid, neither be thou dismayed: for the Lord thy God is with thee whithersoever thou goest"* (Joshua 1:9 KJV).

Remember as we go, we do not battle against flesh and blood. God is Aloha. Aloha each other and all you meet, and aloha the 'āina that God has given to us to care for. Ua Mau Ke Ea O Ka 'Āina I Ka Pono O Iesū Kristo. (The Life of the Land is Perpetuated in the Righteousness of Jesus Christ.)

Aloha Ke Akua,
*Daniel*

# 18
# "The One" Revealed

*'Io-mata-ngaro: His face is hidden and unseen.*

*"And he said, Thou canst not see my face: for there shall no man see me, and live."*

—Exodus 33:20 KJV

A s the time of the 'Io project approached, a supernatural fear fell upon Moke. He did not want to go to his family heiau. He even told Daniel and Landa he changed his mind and was not going.

One day, Moke was walking out the door with his family when the Lord said to him, "*Moke, I want to speak with you,*" so he told his family he needed to stay home. He flipped his Bible open and it opened to Jonah. Moke didn't want to hear about Jonah so he turned the pages to another place and placed the Bible on the window sill. A strong gust of wind suddenly blew through the window and the pages of the Bible began to flip. When Moke looked at it again, it had returned to Jonah! He ignored it and walked away. That night, an elder of the church came to his house to do a Bible study, his message for the night, Jonah! He spoke about how Jonah ran from what God wanted him to do but you cannot run from God. Still stubborn and stiff-necked against going, Moke went to bed. Maybe tomorrow all this weirdness will end he thought. The next morning, Moke went out to get the morning paper, when he opened it, there on the front page was a large picture of a whale breaching! He closed the paper and went out in his car. He turned on the radio to the Christian station, the message for the day, Jonah! Now most people would have gotten the message a long time ago; but not only was this supernatural fear over him, but when Moke made up his mind like this, it was like trying to move a bull that did not want to move. He still would not go.

Daniel and Landa were praying for Moke because they really felt he needed to go to his family heiau, however, they had no idea all of this "Jonah stuff" was happening to him. One afternoon, the Lord gave Landa an order, *"Go to Moke and tell him that if he does not go to 'Iokane, I will spit him up on the shore there like Jonah!"* This was a difficult assignment for Landa. Moke was still a young Christian and still had a lot of the "hard moke" (rough and tough guy) about him. She was scared to give such an order to a big scary guy, but she feared God more. Daniel and Landa asked to see Moke and Pali. When they met, Landa told Moke what the Lord had told her to say. Moke was in shock; the seriousness of this to the Lord became clear to him, and the fear of God finally overcame his fear of going. When Moke shared with Daniel and Landa about all the "Jonah stuff" that had been happening to him, they were shocked in turn. But Moke now knew he must go to 'Iokane and made up his mind to do so.

Moke made an appointment to see his aunt who was the elder kūpuna of the family and who had the key to the gate of the property leading to the heiau. When Moke arrived at his aunt's house, he sat down with her and said, "*Aunty, I feel that I must go to 'Iokāne.*"

"*Why do you want to go there?*" his aunt replied.

"*I must find out what gods we worshipped there. Tell me the truth, Aunty, who did our ancestors worship there?*"

Moke's aunt then called her sons and daughters to come and witness what she was about to say. His aunt's answer shocked them all.

She said, "*Moke, our ancestors were the high priests of 'Io. He is the only true God and creator. We only worshipped Him. Our family sailed from the Middle East to find Hawai'i by the order of our God, 'Io. We arrived in Hawai'i after many generations of sailing and dwelling in different lands. When we finally arrived, we established our family heiau, 'Iokāne, to worship him. We worshipped him in peace for many years.*

"*When Pā'ao came he desecrated 'Iokāne heiau and our family's priestly line to 'Io was cut off. Pā'ao built the human sacrifice heiau on top of the foundations of our temple to 'Io. Pā'ao also placed bloody stones from his home temple in Tahiti, Taputapuatea, the largest and most bloody temple in Polynesia, and from Waha'ula, the first human sacrifice temple that he built in Hawai'i, in the walls of 'Iokane.*

"*Pā'ao was able to do this without a fight because 'Io told your ancestor, the kahuna nui of our heiau, to step down. 'Io spoke a prophecy to him that our family priestly line would be cut off but 'Io also promised that one day our precious family heiau would be restored and rededicated to Him. Someday, someone would be born in the family line who would be 'The One' who would reinstate our priesthood and rededicate 'Iokāne to 'Io.*

"*For many generations our 'ohana (family) waited, longing for 'The One' to come. Moke, when you were young, your grandfather told all of his children he knew who 'The One' would be, although he would not tell us who it was. All of our descendant families wished that one of our children would be 'The One.' It was just before he died that he told us that 'The One' was you, Moke. We never told you because he told us that we must never tell you until the day you came and said you must go to 'Iokāne."* Everyone in the room was weeping now. Moke's aunt told him, *"We always knew 'Io and Jehovah were the same God. The missionaries told us that 'Io was a false god and confused some but we knew that they were one and the same.*

*Go to our heiau, cleanse it and rededicate it to 'Io. Pray and 'Io will show you what to do. Go!"*

That evening, Moke and Pali, dazed and excited, shared with Daniel and Landa what had transpired. Daniel and Landa were shocked. They could not believe what they were hearing. All of them felt like they were living in a Bible story that God had given them the privilege to live in. Walking out God's directions step by step, none of them had ever dreamed that the 'Io Project would be about fulfilling God's 800-year-old prophecy!

'Iokāne was at the center of a tentacle of heiau(s) and high places that crossed the southern islands of Hawai'i (the Big Island), Maui and Moloka'i. This major tentacle went from Waha'ula, the first luakini heiau, over the top of Mauna Kea, the highest mountain in Hawai'i, over the top of the Kohala mountains, over 'Iokāne, across the ocean to Maui, over the top of Haleakalā, over the heiau at Honokōhau Valley on the head of Maui, and across the ocean to Hālawa Valley, Moloka'i, the area with the highest concentration of luakini heiau in all of Hawai'i.

Moke and Pali told Daniel and Landa that, because of prior commitments, the earliest they could arrive at 'Iokāne was 3:00 p.m. Daniel wondered why this was so. He knew by faith that God works all things for good for those that love Him and are called to His purposes, but why 3:00 p.m.? Most of the teams were going to their assigned heiau(s) at first light. It was Beth Naholowaʻa Murph again who later found the answer: 3:00 p.m. is the ninth hour of the Jewish day; this was the time of the evening prayer and sacrifice. It was also the time the Passover Lamb was slain on the 14th day. It was in the ninth hour that Jesus died on the cross. It was also when the thick and heavy curtain of the temple (which separated the people from the Holy of Holies where the presence of God dwelt) was rent from top to bottom, symbolically setting the people free to enter into the Holy of Holies to have a personal relationship with God.

It was also clear that this heiau had to be taken last, not only because of its strategic location, but because of its significance as the ancient Hawaiian high temple to ʻIo. This temple could not be rededicated to ʻIo until the tentacles of human sacrifice and worship of Taʻaroa were repented of and forgiven by God across the islands. As the tentacles of Taʻaroa are lifted from the land across the island chain, this temple, the ʻāina (the land and nature) and the Hawaiian people could again be rededicated to the God they served before the desecration by Pāʻao— this time, returning to ʻIo through Iesū Kristo (Jesus Christ) his Son!

That night, Daniel thanked the Lord for asking him to take on the ʻIo Project. Wasn't it just like his God? His God had a sense of humor and also was omnipotent! He had orchestrated the many events throughout Hawaiian history, Moke's life, Daniel's life and the lives of the other people involved in the ʻIo Project to all fall into place for this one moment in time! Daniel had thought that God was asking him to detour away from of his calling in ministry; instead, it turned out to be a greater breakthrough in his area of ministry than anything he could have ever dreamed of! Daniel imagined God laughing as He watched him trudge along, being the good martyr for God and feeling sorry for himself, when all along God knew the wonderful surprise He had in store for him. Daniel praised his Lord with an overwhelming joy. He served such a good and great God!

After 800 years, "The One" had finally come!

# 19

# Kehilat O Ka Mesia

*'Io-matua-kore: He had no parents,*
*"He was nothing but himself."*

*Yahweh (Hebrew): meaning—*
*The Self-Existent One.*

*"I AM THAT I AM."*
—Exodus 3:14 KJV

## Kaua'i

Ben, the congregational leader of Kehilat O Ka Mesia, was troubled. Even though Daniel said the Lord wanted the 'Io Project done on the 14th of March, Purim by the Jewish calendar was actually on the Thursday and Friday before the 14th. Ben couldn't shake the feeling that their team needed to do their part of the work on the actual days by the Jewish calendar. He knew Daniel said the Lord told him it needed to be done at one time. Was he being disobedient or was he hearing from God? Finally, Ben called Daniel, shared with him his concerns, and asked if Kehilat O Ka Mesia could do their part on Thursday and Friday, the 12th and 13th of March.

"*I knew we had to pray about this,*" said Daniel. "*Would this alert the forces of darkness to our plan? We had been praying all this time that God would blind the eyes of the enemy from what we were doing. Was this really God impressing Ben to do this?*"

After praying with Landa, they both felt God was speaking to Ben. The 12th was also the day the Worldwide Prayer Shield for Hawai'i was to begin. He called Ben and gave him their blessing to go ahead with their part of the 'Io Project on the 12th and 13th of March, Purim by the Jewish calendar.

They all prayed that Ben had heard correctly and that the Kehilat O Ka Mesia team would be protected as they went out early alone. They also prayed that they did not make a mistake that would jeopardize the entire 'Io Project. Only time would tell what would happen.

# 20
# The Mountain Ridge

*'Io-te-waiora: He is the source and giver of life.*

*"For with thee is the fountain of life."*

— Psalm 36:9 KJV

Landa Kikawa had a vision that she and Daniel were to go to the top of the mountain ridge on the island of Moloka'i above Hālawa Valley. In her vision, she saw where they needed to go on the morning of March 14; it was marked by a large dead tree.

It was no surprise that God would direct them to be on Moloka'i for the opening of the 'Io Project. In ancient times, the kahuna(s) of Moloka'i were feared as the most powerful in the islands. Though it is the second smallest of the major islands, Moloka'i had 17 known human sacrifice heiau(s) while the island next to it, Lana'i, which was nearly the same size, had only one! Nine of the 17 are in Hālawa Valley where the most powerful kahuna(s) of Moloka'i dwelt. Hālawa Valley and the valleys of Northeastern Moloka'i are the eroded side of an ancient volcano. They were to go to the rim of the volcano above Hālawa Valley.

The sides of the volcano are steep wilderness forest reserves. The top of the mountain ridges for many miles around Hālawa Valley on the south side are nearly inaccessible, entailing a long and difficult hike along goat and deer trails. Only a few on Moloka'i, the most experienced hunters, have ever been to this remote area.

On the north side, it was even more inaccessible. It looked like the Ko'olau Mountains on the windward side of O'ahu: sheer green cliffs rising into the clouds. This area was said to have the highest sea cliffs in the world, rising 3000 feet above the waves.

There were two choices to get to the top of the mountain and both were difficult and potentially dangerous: The first option would be to hike there. Experienced hunters told Daniel it would take at least six hours to get there by hiking up the south side of the mountain following narrow deer trails. Being inexperienced hikers, Daniel figured that Landa and he would take at least two hours longer than that. "This meant we would not get back down the valley in time to return to the Big Island," said Daniel. "The Lord had spoken strongly to my heart that we needed to be at 'Iokāne heiau at 3:00 p.m. the same day. This is when Moke would fulfill the prophecy. Because we needed to be there, hiking was out."

The second option was to go by helicopter. There were several problems with this method: the ridge is full of trees and, because it is very steep, there are not many places to land. Most pilots would not even attempt it. It was also a forest reserve and to get permits to land there would take a long time. Next, prohibitive cost. The best price that Daniel found was $1,050 an hour plus $250 an hour if the pilot had to wait for them.

Through friends, they obtained permission to land on property that was half way up the mountain. This would cut the hiking time in half. Daniel calculated it would take two hours' flying time to and from Hilo, plus six to eight hours to hike to the top of the mountain and back; then they would also need to add time to pray there. They were looking at a minimum cost of well over $3,000, more than Daniel and Landa could afford. They found out that this helicopter company was booked anyway. As they made more calls, they discovered all the helicopters were booked that day. Even if they had the money and the helicopter was available, they still could not make it back to ʻIokāne heiau by 3:00 p.m. It was over an hour's drive from the nearest working airport to where the trail to ʻIokāne heiau began.

There seemed to be no solution. All Daniel and Landa could say was, "*Lord we do this in obedience to you. We have done all we can. The rest is up to you. If we are really hearing you correctly and you really want us to go to both places, you need to make a way for us to fulfill what you have asked us to do.*"

Thursday morning, March 12, dawned; and Daniel was still without a solution to their dilemma. The phone rang; it was Jacob Mau on Maui. Jacob was known as the best search-and-rescue man on Maui. He had hunted the mountains and back country of Maui since he was a boy and knew the land like his own back yard. He was a major factor in helping the Maui team find several heiau(s). Jacob told Daniel he was helping Pastor Alan Cravallo get permits to go into several remote valleys in Hamakua on the Big Island. So Daniel told him of their unsolvable problem on Molokaʻi. Jacob said he would see what he could do and call him back. Daniel didn't have high hopes. He had already checked out every possible option. But an hour later, Jacob called back, "*I got you a helicopter that will land you at the very top of the mountain - FREE!*" Daniel was stunned. It turned out Jacob had a pilot friend, Mike, who owed him a favor. He and Jacob had worked together many times doing search-and-rescue missions. Getting permits was not a problem for these search-and-rescue pilots. Jacob said Mike was the best pilot in the islands and that he had landed in the Moloka'i high country many times. God only provides the best! When Jacob asked his friend to take Daniel and Landa to Moloka'i, Mike showed Jacob his appointment book. He said, "*Look, I was booked solid on Saturday but EVERY SINGLE ONE OF THEM CANCELLED. I will take your friends anywhere they want to go.*"

Daniel and Landa were giddy with amazement and joy at God's provision. He did want them to go to both places. The 'Io project was only two days away and they were ready.

# 21
# Purim

"Behold, the day cometh, that shall burn as an oven; and
all the proud, yea, and all that do wickedly, shall be stubble... ²But unto you that fear my name shall the **Sun of
Righteousness** arise with healing in his wings; and ye shall go
forth, and grow up as calves of the stall. ³And ye shall tread
down the wicked; for they shall be ashes under the soles of your
feet in the day that I shall do this, saith the LORD of hosts."

—Malachi 4:1-3 KJV

## Kaua'i

As the group from Kehilat O Ka Mesia sought the Lord
as to where he would lead them, they looked at a map
of Kaua'i and saw something they had never noticed before.
There on the map was the Hebrew letter, *Shin,* created by the
mountains and valleys of Kaua'i. This Hebrew letter is very
significant in Judaism. The letter Shin is shaped like a three
pronged root with its fingers pointing upwards, lifted to heaven.
Shin represents the Shema, the watchword in Judaism, "Hear
O Israel, the Lord our God is One Lord" (Deut. 6:4 KJV). This

letter, representing the Presence of the Almighty, appears on the doorposts of Jewish homes in the form of the Mezuzah. Just as in earthly realms, a root grows downward and gains its sustenance from the earth, the Shin's "roots" point to heaven to receive its sustenance from God. As they looked at the Shin on the map, its base was the summit of Mount Wai'ale'ale. The Spirit of the Lord then impressed on Ben clearly that on Thursday, March 12, the first day of Purim in the Jewish calendar, they needed to go to the summit of Wai'ale'ale.

The island of Kaua'i is roughly the shape of a circle. Unlike the other Hawaiian islands, it has one central mountain, Wai'ale'ale. Although the heiau on the Wai'ale'ale summit was not a known luakini heiau, Ben felt it was significant for three reasons:

1. It was the highest point on Kaua'i. High places have always held great power in physical and spiritual warfare. The Lord spoke to teams on other islands about going to the highest place on those islands. There was a team going to the summit of Haleakalā on Maui, Beth and Tim Murph's team was going to the summit of Mauna Kea on the Big Island and Daniel and Yolanda were going to the top of the mountain range over Hālawa Valley on Moloka'i.

2. Wai'ale'ale was one of the farthest places on earth from Jerusalem, and the Gospel needed to go to the "ends of the earth" (Acts 1:8).

3. Wai'ale'ale is the wettest spot on earth. Thus, when the Gospel reached this place, "the ends of the earth," it would precipitate a revival which would now begin to flow back (rains/water representing the Spirit of Revival) and return to Jerusalem in the form of the nations helping restore the Messiah to the Jewish people (Romans 11).

As Ben started doing research, he found it was all but "impossible" to get to the summit of Wai'ale'ale. All he heard was, *"You can't get a permit," "You can't go up there," "Helicopters won't land there,"* etc. At that time, and even at this writing, permits to drop off people at the summit of Wai'ale'ale were and are not now being issued. They began to pray and both Ben and Lydia heard, *"Stand back and see the salvation of the Lord."*

Helicopter pilots avoid the summit of Wai'ale'ale because of its heavy rains. The mountain receives average annual rainfall of 451 inches. As water-laden clouds blow in from the ocean, they are pushed upward against the slopes until they pour out their rain. Unlike the other islands with several mountains, no matter where the wind blew from, it would drive the clouds up this one central mountain. The summit of Wai'ale'ale is rarely visible because of these constant rain clouds. These wet conditions also make hiking the mountain a grueling ordeal. For those brave enough to try it, there are two ways to the summit of Wai'ale'ale. One is a long and winding trail up from Waimea Canyon and Koke'e State Park and the other is by following Wailua stream since there is no trail from that side. Any way you went, it was wet and treacherous at places and thigh-deep mud at others. Very few people on Kaua'i have ever been to the summit. It is considered inaccessible except to the most experienced hikers, and it can take several days to hike up and back down. Ben was told that many people had become lost hiking on the mountain and had spent wet, mosquito-filled nights hunkered down in mud bogs. He saw that, for all practical purposes, Wai'ale'ale was inaccessible by foot to their inexperienced group. He began searching for a helicopter to take them in.

Then came their first big answer to prayer. The Dept. of Land and Natural Resources called to say they decided to give them a permit! The person on the phone said, *"You will*

*get your permit in time and will go up there."* Ben and Lydia
realized the Lord was giving them a small window of time,
Purim, to go to the mountain and do what He desired done.
It was all God! So, they moved quickly to hire a helicopter.
The first company they procured a helicopter from cancelled
out on them for some unknown reason two days before they
were to depart. The helicopter companies were so busy, Ben
didn't know if he could find another one in time. He called
another company and this one said, "No problem. *We did it
before."* Not only that, they got the best pilot on the island.
God always provides the best!

Because the helicopter schedule was so full, they were only
given a 30-minute window of time to do what they needed
to do. When they subtracted the flight time, they would have
only 20 minutes on the summit of Wai'ale'ale. The team prepared by praying, asking God to fulfill all he wanted done in
this short time.

Pastor Vil Galiza was the long-time Pastor of Aloha
Church. He had always felt that Wai'ale'ale held a key to
revival on Kaua'i. He felt it so strongly that several times he
had tried to get to the summit but things always fell through.
Vil decided it was not God's timing. Knowing this, Ben asked
Pastor Vil to go with them, and he was thrilled!

On Thursday, March 12, Ben, Kepola, Pastor Vil and a
Hawaiian woman, Mahina, were on their way up to Wai'ale'ale
in the helicopter. The flight was smooth and beautiful. But
as they approached the mountain, they saw massive clouds
swirling around the summit. The pilot informed them that,
unless there was a break in the clouds, it would be too dangerous to land. There was a point of demarcation, a point at
which, if it was not clear, they would have to turn back. The
pilot would not risk getting too close to the mountain with
low visibility. The little team began to pray.

Soon they were flying through the clouds; there was heavy cloud cover everywhere they looked. Just as they reached the demarcation line where the pilot would have to turn back, he pointed and said, "*Look! I can see the peak. The peak is clear!*" There were clouds everywhere but just at that point in time, the clouds parted and a window-shaped opening in the clouds appeared! The Window of Time! The pilot expertly guided the helicopter through the window in the clouds to the summit landing area. This pilot knew exactly where the heiau on the summit crater was; he had taken an eagle feather there once, a gift from a Native American.

As they prepared to land, this vanguard team expected a demonic war with the Lord of Darkness. Ben said, "*I thought we would have our hair standing up on end, but we only felt peace.*" Like Israel's army facing the enemy in 2 Kings 7, the enemy had already fled by the hand of God. The Lord had prepared the way for them; they just needed to walk out their assignment.

As the pilot hovered over the site, the team prepared to spring into action. They had brought a shofar (a Hebrew ram's horn) and a conch shell, the Hawaiian counterpart. These are both blown as a call to worship, to war, and for special assemblies. Ben wore Hebrew garments and had brought a torah scroll. The torah held the five books of Moses, Genesis through Deuteronomy, in Hebrew. Kepola and Mahina were in their Native Hawaiian garments. They had brought unleavened bread and kosher wine with them. The team represented Israel, the first, Hawai'i, the last, and Vil, who is of Filipino descent, the nations of the world.

The pilot landed smoothly on a clear summit and they announced their arrival with the blowing of the shofar and conch shells. Kepola sang a song about the Hawai'i state motto, "*Ua mau ke ea o ka ʻāina i ka pono*" which means, "*The life of the land is perpetuated in righteousness"* accompanied by the ipu heke (Hawaiian gourd drum) and prayers. They then prayed at the heiau for the people of Hawai'i and the people of Israel. As Kepola knelt at the heiau, deep uwē(s), cries of mourning, began to shake her body, pouring uncontrollably forth from her na'au (her innermost being) as she repented for the hewa (the sins) of her people. She asked 'Io for mercy, forgiveness and cleansing in the name of His son, Iesū.

The team had brought a scarf that contained the tears of Lydia, Ben's wife, shed for the Hawaiian people and the people of Israel. This scarf of tears was dipped into the sacred pond in the crater at the summit. They broke bread and asked 'Io's blessing on the island and its people. They poured some of the kosher wine and planted some of the unleavened bread on the earth. They prayed that from Hawai'i, the last, revival would start and return to Israel, the first.

The team felt so privileged to be there. Few people had set foot on this mountaintop, but the Lord made a way for them to come at just the right time. The clouds stayed right on the rim of the peak the whole time. The team left the summit praising God and believing they had taken out the first major stronghold of Ta'aroa. The other assignments would go easier because of it.

Wai'ale'ale means "rippling waters". The rains on Wai'ale'ale stream down to all areas of Kaua'i and fill its artesian water system. These waters are the source of life for the whole island. Upon her return, Kepola wrote a song about Wai'ale'ale and the cleansing rain soon to come.[1]

―――――

On Friday, March 13, the Kehilat O Ka Mesia team, this time without pastor Vil but now including Kepola's husband, Iokepa, went to their assigned heiau. The name of this heiau meant, "*Closed Out to the Light.*" As they arrived, they sensed immediately that this had been a foreboding spiritual stronghold in the past. At the entrance to the heiau were two trees. One was bent at an angle against the other making a doorway entrance to the heiau. In Jewish tradition, a mezuzah (a small container which holds the scripture Deut. 6:4-9) is to be attached to the doorpost of the doorway. Ben did not attach a physical mezuzah to this "doorpost" but did so "in the spirit."

In Jewish tradition, they put the kosher wine they brought on the doorposts and lintel, which represented the protection of the blood Jesus shed for them. This tradition began when Moses and the people of Israel were in Egypt and the spirit of death saw the blood of the sacrificial lamb on their doorways and passed over.

As Ben was praying, he felt that Kepola, the one who had chiefly Hawaiian blood, should lead. They blew the conch and shofar in protocol before entering. As they entered through the doorway, they realized how massive this heiau was. It had four large rectangle platforms in tiers that rose higher and higher. The platforms overlooked a cliff over the ocean. As this strange team, in their Hawaiian and Jewish garments with Ben again carrying a torah entered in, they sensed tremendous pain; the land seemed to be crying out in anguish at the innocent bloodshed.

The team prayed at each level. The sky was dark and covered with clouds, but each time they finished praying, a beam of light shone upon them, like a signal that their prayers were answered. It seemed as if 'Io was saying, "*This place that was 'Closed Out to the Light,' is now 'Open to the Light!'*"

As they finished praying and headed toward the entrance of the heiau, they went in reverse order. Kepola was now the last. As Kepola passed out of the doorway of trees, in Jewish tradition, she touched the mezuzah. Instantly, a beam of sunlight, like a laser, pierced the thick clouds, lighting up the top of Kepola's head like a halo and continuing onto her hand that was touching the mezuzah! Kepola froze. The others turned, saw it and were amazed. The beam of light seemed supernaturally bright and remained upon her for some time as Kepola alternately laughed in joy at the goodness and faithfulness of God and wept at His great love for her. She described what she experienced as *"being immersed in God's Glory!"* The others were laughing and crying, too. They could see and sense the Spirit of God all over her! It was a most glorious day!

As they were walking out, they found the gate locked. Iokepa stepped forward, touched the lock, and it fell open. The team felt they were living a Bible story! They read about things like this happening in the Bible, but had never lived it. It was a picture of what God did that day; He unlocked the doors to set people free.

The vanguard of the 'Io Project had completed their tasks successfully. Would the rest of the 'Io Project go as well? The Kehilat O Ka Mesia team dedicated themselves to pray for the main assault upon the stronghold of the Prince of Darkness, Ta'aroa.

# 22

# Friday, March 13— The Day Before the 'Io Project

*Connected to the fall of the first man and woman was an animal called the Mo'opeloa. Mo'opeloa means The Serpent of Lies or Flattery (Mo'o - serpent, lizard or reptile and pelo - to flatter, tell tall tales or lie).*

*Many ancient mariners thought they saw a sea serpent, when actually what they saw were the twisting tentacles of a giant squid.*

## Pastor Alan Cravalho
## Honoka'a, Big Island

Pastor Alan Cravalho, along with George and Tammy Ruiz, had been preparing for their mission in Waimanu Valley with fasting and prayer. George and Tammy were newcomers to Honoka'a. King's Cathedral Maui had sent George to help its Honoka'a extension church as worship leader. George had accepted Pastor Alan's invitation to go with him on his adventure, but he reminded him he was a musician not a hiker. Pastor Alan assured him they were going in by helicopter. Even if they weren't it was hard to say no to Pastor Alan.

George and Pastor Alan seem like polar opposites. Alan is wide bodied and intense; George is slender and laid back. Besides the Lord, the biggest thing they had in common was their humor. It was a guarantee that if you hung out with them you would end up laughing. They had a real Dean Martin and Jerry Lewis thing going. They had no clue how much they would need their sense of humor.

At 2:30 a.m. on Friday, March 13, Tammy awoke with the worst asthma attack she had had in many years. George took one look at his wife and drove her to the Emergency Room. Tammy and George felt that this was just another attack of the enemy to stop them from their mission; they were not going to let this stop Tammy from going. She had taken some medical tests and was waiting for her asthma medicine when the doctor returned and said, *"You may be pregnant. We need to do a pregnancy test to make sure before giving you the medication."*

George and Tammy were flabbergasted. Tammy was 38 and their last child was born 17 years before. They thought they were done having children. Like Sarah in the Bible who laughed when the angel told her she would bear a son in her old age, Tammy and George laughed it off too. There was no way. What popped into their remembrance however were the words of a prophet who had come to their church three months before. George had been away on a business trip at the time, and Tammy was in church by herself. The prophet had looked at Tammy and said, *"Where is your husband."* Tammy told the prophet George was away. The prophet then said, *"Tell your husband that within the next three months you will be pregnant."* When George got home, they had had a good laugh about it.

The doctor returned. *"Well, you are two months pregnant!"* Tammy and George could not believe it but were overjoyed at having this promised child. Little did they realize what providence it was to find out Tammy was pregnant before March 14.

---

## John Kūpuna
## Hālawa Valley, Molokaʻi

John Kūpuna was in his element, walking the ʻāina of his beloved Hālawa Valley, the land of his youth. Before setting out, he charted the location of each heiau and calculated how long it would take to reach them. He had received much favor from the people of the land. He had gone in proper Hawaiian style and asked permission of everyone whose land they must cross. When they heard why he was going to the heiau(s), many were blessed by it and told him to go for it. Now at a sparkling fresh-water pond he had visited often in his youth, John dove for prawns.

---

## Pastor Alan Cravalho
## Honokaʻa, Big Island

On the afternoon of Friday March 13, Pastor Alan was still in the library getting historical information about Waimanu Valley and the heiau(s) there. He had been very late in applying for a permit to land a helicopter in Waimanu Valley. A few days earlier the Department of Land and Natural Resources told him there was no way he could get a helicopter permit on such short notice. Besides, the person who took care of these permits was away. Pastor Alan decided not to tell George this. He was still believing for the impossible. He had been so sure

God was going to get a helicopter for them that he had not even made other contingency plans.

When the Department of Land and Natural Resources had called to tell Pastor Alan he couldn't get a helicopter permit, he had contacted Nalani Subiono to check on getting a Zodiac boat for them to go in by sea, just as a backup plan. Nalani had secured a boat, but called back later to say the company had suddenly cancelled on them. Meanwhile, Pastor Alan took out a hiking permit for Waimanu Valley. *It's just as a precaution—a backup thing*—he told himself. He couldn't imagine God would be asking him to hike in. The winding, nine-mile trail into Waimanu Valley traversed 13 gulches, 13 streams and 12 steep ridges. To hike in and out in one day meant hiking a grueling 18 miles across 26 gulches, 26 streams and 24 ridges! The "Muliwai" trail into Waimanu Valley began with an arduous 1200 foot ascent up the Waipiʻo Valley cliff on a switchback trail. It then traversed an obstacle course of gulches and ridges of up to 500 feet before descending another 1200 feet into Waimanu Valley.

The ease or difficulty of hiking an area is relative to the person attempting it. For an experienced hiker, mountain or rock climber, in great shape and with the right equipment, the hike into Waimanu Valley may seem easy; but for Pastor Alan, George and Tammy, this hike would be extremely difficult and potentially deadly.

So much also depended on the weather and trail conditions. This area of the Big Island receives over 100 inches of rain annually. It is a common occurrence for the Hāmakua Coast Highway to be closed because of rock slides; the potential for rock slides over the trail to Waimanu Valley was much greater. If the trail had not been maintained recently (it was only minimally maintained) it could be very dangerous for a novice hiker. An inexperienced hiker climbing over a steep rockslide of loose rocks on a cliff trail was asking for trouble. The sign at the entrance to Waipi'o Valley warned that the Muliwai trail to Waimanu Valley was *"steep, deeply eroded in places, rocky, muddy, and slippery when wet."* The sign also warned that *"only experienced hikers in good physical condition should attempt it."*

If it was raining, the sign warned that there was the danger of flash flooding in the 13 streams they would need to cross. It said that attempting to cross the streams when it was raining was *"potentially fatal."*

Yes, hiking was an absolute last resort. Pastor Alan had no intention whatsoever of hiking in there. Still hoping for a miracle, Pastor Alan called one last time and found out he still couldn't get a helicopter permit. The more Pastor Alan looked at the maps the afternoon of March 13, the more he couldn't believe what he was about to do. He had been so sure they were going to fly in, pray, praise God, then fly out and get to 'Iokāne by 3 p.m. Now he began to consider the awful prospect that God may *want* them to hike in. The reality that they would have to make that grueling hike finally began to set in. Giving up because they could not get a helicopter or boat was never an option. He was going in, failure was not an option. And when Pastor Alan made up his mind, he made up his mind.

That afternoon, Pastor Alan's wife, Delfin, and George's wife, Tammy, learned from their friend Louise that there definitely would not be a helicopter. Tammy had still been planning to go into Waimanu Valley. When she found out there would be no helicopter and they would have to hike in, she knew she couldn't go. Now that she was pregnant, she couldn't take the risk of such a long and dangerous hike. It was the providence of God that she found out she was pregnant just before March 14. Tammy was out of this mission; it would be Pastor Alan and George hiking in alone. Delfin asked Louise, *"Is this a safe area for inexperienced hikers?*

*Shouldn't there be a minimum of three of them going in there?"* Louise was silent. Delfin felt uneasy. She kept hearing "No, no, no." in her spirit. "NO," if there were only two. She had to confront Pastor Alan about this. Delfin could be hard-headed too; she had to be to be married to Pastor Alan!

Pastor Alan planned to start hiking at 3:30 a.m. based on information he got from a hunter who had hiked several times into the area between Waipi'o and Waimanu valleys. *"Three hours,"* the hunter had said, *"gets you into Waimanu by 6:30."* Pastor Alan may have wanted to believe this "rosy" scenario of the time it would take not wanting to see what they would really have to face. He overlooked asking this person if he ever went all the way into the valley in one day, what the condition of the trail was at the time, and many other important questions. Based on this information, Pastor Alan figured on five hours' hiking time just to be safe. That would get them there by 8:30. Pastor Alan had been fasting and praying since Sunday evening. That Friday he had gotten up to pray at 3:30 a.m. These things prepared his spirit for the battle ahead, but not his body. After fasting for five days and having little sleep, he now was faced with having to wake up at 2:30 a.m. He had not hiked even a walking trail in 20 years and had never been in this valley or hiked anywhere on this island since he had come from Maui. He had no hiking gear or boots. He knew people had died in there and others had been lost. Daniel had friends whose son was lost in the area and never found. Another friend of a friend had fallen off a cliff and died. Pastor Alan heard that on the steep and slippery trail along the cliff to Waimanu Valley, even mules had fallen off! Yet, the thought of giving up never entered his mind.

Both Delfin Cravalho and Tammy Ruiz felt such uneasiness and heaviness as they prayed for their husbands. They knew their men were inexperienced hikers and way out of shape for a trek like this. However, it was the spiritual dangers that were even more concerning to them than the physical ones. Their husbands would be entering the stronghold of one of the most powerful principalities in the islands with the intent of destroying his power. This supernaturally powerful entity would not take this lying down! They needed to make sure this was all in God's plan and under his protection. They asked their friend Ty to pray with them and to give them her counsel. Ty's husband, Delbert, was from Honoka'a and had been an avid hunter. He had hunted in Waimanu Valley several times, although not in many years. Ty knew it could be a dangerous place, especially for novices. She did not feel good about Pastor Alan and George going into the valley alone. With Tammy and Ty's confirmation of her feelings, Delfin decided she was not going to let her husband go on this journey without a third person who was an experienced hiker and who knew the valley well. She was going to make a stand that night.

---

## Moke

Moke had never been to his family heiau of 'Iokāne but during times of prayer 'Io showed him visions of what it would look like and what he must do to cleanse it. 'Io told him only four people were to enter the heiau for the cleansing. He could see three of them—himself, Kahu Gaymond Apaka (Moke's cousin and pastor), and Daniel Kikawa. In the vision there was a fourth person but Moke could not see his face. He was praying about this when 'Io spoke to him and said, "*You will know him when you see him.*" Moke was now at peace about this. God would show him who it was when the time came. He was ready.

---

### Pastor Alan Cravalho
### Honoka'a, Big Island

Pastor Alan really needed to keep his positive focus to be ready for the battle ahead. He did not need "Job's comforters" at this time. *"Don't be foolish!"* Delfin scolded him at dinner Friday evening.

*"You need to go with someone who knows the area well and this type of terrain. You have never hiked anywhere on this island since you got here and this is one of the most inaccessible and dangerous areas to hike!"*

Pastor Alan, still fasting, just drank his juice and would not listen to her.

She finally said, *"No! You are not going! Not unless you have someone who knows the area with you. We need to be in agreement and we are not!"*

Delfin was adamant and Pastor Alan was just as stubborn. Their 11-year-old realizing his dad was going into a dangerous situation started crying. Their 14-year-old said, *"Dad, if you take anyone, you gotta take Uncle Delbert."*

Pastor Alan had talked with Delbert about the trip but just to get information about Waimanu, not about hiking into it. He didn't want to bring Delbert because it "made sense." He wanted it to be a "God idea," not a "man idea." This was to protect Delbert. He knew the seriousness of what they were going to do. He didn't want Delbert to get hurt.

———

It wasn't until 9:00 p.m. on Friday night after worship practice that George found out they were going to have to hike in. George thought, *"As usual, always the last to know!"* George later said, if he knew fully what he was getting into, he would never have gone and would have missed out on one of the greatest blessings of his life. Pastor Alan took out the map and quickly traced where they needed to go.

"Well, first we drive into Waipi'o valley, here. Then, we cross over the Waipi'o River here in the middle of the valley floor. After that we just hike up the wall of the Waipi'o mountain ridge here (George noticed that he didn't say cliff) and then we just go across this area here to Waimanu." Pastor Alan was already folding away the map when he mentioned to George in the most matter-of-fact way, "We need to get up at 2:30 a.m. to go. It will take about three hours to hike in and three hours out."

Now Pastor Alan was not lying to George about the hiking time. Pastor Alan would never do that. Let's just say he asked several people how long it took to get there, and one person said about three hours in and three out so he decided to tell George the best scenario. Besides, Pastor Alan wanted to believe it would be that easy himself.

George began to feel a creeping uneasiness about this "adventure." George began to pray even harder. He did not realize that he, Delfin, Tammy and Ty were all praying the same thing, "God, can you convince Delbert to go, too?"

———

9 years later, Daniel found much more information about the Muliwai trail and Waimanu Valley that was not available in 1998. There are now many websites and books that mention this hike. Even though the trail is much better maintained now, most of these sources said that this hike will take about 9 hours going in and 10+ hours coming back out, and even hard-core hikers should not attempt it in one day. The fastest time mentioned that Daniel could find was 7 hours one way. The most detailed book about the trail said that the final 1200 foot descent into Waimanu Valley was "poorly maintained and extremely hazardous... The trail is very narrow and washed out in parts, with sheer drop-offs hundreds of feet into the ocean, and nothing to hold onto apart from mossy rocks and spiny plants. Dense leaves underfoot hide centipedes

*and slippery kukui [nuts]. If the descent proves impossible, head back…"*[1] It is a good thing that this information was not available to George. He would have never gone!

---

### Daniel and Landa

When Daniel heard from Moke that God wanted him to be one of the four to cleanse 'Iokāne he was amazed. No wonder he felt so strongly that he needed to get back from Moloka'i that same day! Daniel and Landa arrived on Maui the night of March 13 to rest before catching their helicopter to Moloka'i. They were met by Jacob and Maryann Mau. As they were driving to the Kikawas' hotel, Maryann talked about how blessed they were to have this particular pilot. *"Mike is the best pilot in the islands!"* she gushed, *"He has crashed seven times, he is the best crasher!"* Landa and Daniel looked at her, stunned. *"No! I mean he really knows how to crash! Uhh, when he gets in trouble, he crashes really well. Oh, this just isn't coming out right is it?"* She was trying to say that, if they got into trouble, if any pilot could take them down safely it was Mike. His seven crash landings were made during the Vietnam War and while flying as a search-and-rescue/drug enforcement pilot. Daniel and Landa had never flown on a helicopter before. This information was not reassuring for their first time! Landa just looked at Daniel. Her look said, *"If not for God, there is no way I would go up there!"*

---

### Pastor Alan Cravalho
### Honoka'a, Big Island

George was exhausted. He had taken Tammy to the Emergency Room at 2:30 a.m. on March 13 and then went to morning prayer at 5:30 a.m. It had been a long day, and he had no chance to sleep. Now he was facing a long hike on short rest. It was nearly 10:00 p.m. and all George wanted to do was get to bed. He was on his fifth day of fasting, had only a few hours of sleep over the last two days and was taking antibiotics for a nasal infection. Maybe he could get more than three hours of sleep before he had to get up again for their hike. Just then the phone rang. *"Who would be calling so late?"* he thought.

*"Aye bra, it's Delbert."* Ty had been nagging Delbert all night to call George or Pastor Alan. Delbert did not even want to talk to them. He wanted no chance of their getting him into a corner where he felt obligated to go. Delbert had been squirming and bobbing and weaving all night. He had never hiked in and out of that place in one day. When he had gone hunting there before, they had always made camp half way in and spent a few days hunting in the area before coming out. For inexperienced, out of shape hikers to go all the way into Waimanu Valley and come all the way back out in the same day was just crazy! He was in no mood to destroy his body in what he knew would be a grueling 14+ hour sprint up and down treacherous cliffs on short notice. Besides, it had been at least three or four years since he had been in there. But after an evening of praying, pleading and nagging, Ty finally got Delbert to call George. Delbert called, but he was not a happy camper. His purpose was to persuade them not to go. There was no way Delbert wanted to do this hike, especially without any preparation. George said later, *"That was Delbert's mistake, he called!"*

"Bra!" said Delbert, *"You know what you doing or what? Going be seven hours going in only, Bra!"* Both Delbert and George could speak "Mainland English." But like most local guys, they slipped into Hawaiian pidgin when talking with each other.

"Well, Pasta when show me da map and when say, 'Oh, yeah, we gotta go here. About three hours in 'an three out."

Delbert's silence made George feel more uneasy. In his mind swirled all the reasons he shouldn't go: he was out of shape, he was sick and on antibiotics, he hadn't had any sleep, he had been fasting, and he was totally unprepared. It was nearly 10 p.m. and there was no way was he going to sleep now with so much stuff going on in his head!

"I tink you gotta come wit us," said George.

"Oh, bra, sorry, I cannot go, my wife get plenty tings she like me do tomorrow," Delbert apologized. In the background George could hear Ty yelling, "He can go wit you! He can go wit you!"

"Rats!" Delbert thought, "Rats! Just what I was trying to avoid!" He was trapped! "Bra, you know what time you gotta go?"

"Yea, Pasta wen say 3:30 a.m. we start walking."

"No, Bra, to get out by dark, you gotta go NOW!"

"You mean right now?"

"Yea, right now, bra!"

George saw Tammy's eyes get large as saucers. He could see she was praying and pleading with God to help Delbert say, "Yes."

"Rats!" Ty trapped him like a rat! Finally and very, very reluctantly, Delbert consented to go with them. The wives immediately felt the peace of God fall over them. They knew they still needed to pray, but they felt so relieved. They sensed that all was pono now, and when you were in right order with God, there was nothing to fear!

# 23
# March 14

*"Ye shall not need to fight in this battle: set yourselves, stand ye still, and see the Salvation of the Lord..."*

—2 Chronicles 20 :17a KJV

*Pastor Alan Cravalho*
*Waimanu Valley, Big Island*

Pastor Alan, George and Delbert left for Waimanu Valley at 10:30 p.m. on March 13. The wives could see the anointing of God upon them and finally felt at peace. They knew they still needed to pray them through this journey so Ty, Delfin and Tammy agreed to take turns praying throughout the night.

By the time the men reached the floor of Waipi'o Valley it was 11:00 p.m. George, an amateur hiker, had overloaded his pack with 50 pounds of food, water and supplies. So by the time they reached the river he was already tired. Unlike George, Pastor Alan knew how to prepare for a long hike. He had been a National Park ranger in the early '70s but because he hadn't done any hiking in 20 years, he had no hiking gear. He was overweight, out of shape, on his fifth day of fasting, and wearing cross-trainer sneakers. George had come dressed in a tank top and shorts. He didn't own hiking boots, and all the stores were closed by the time he learned they were going in by foot. He came wearing a pair of fishing tabis (tah-bees), which are like socks with a thin rubber sole attached to them. Tabis are made for walking on flat reefs, not for hiking! They provided no ankle support and very little foot protection. Already George could feel every rock he stepped on. He would feel every root, rock and kukui nut on the path of their 18-mile hike. They were a sorry sight. Delbert was thinking, *"What amateurs! I must be crazy taking them in. They probably won't make it and then what; I can't carry them out, especially Pastor Alan!"* If it weren't for that, Delbert would have had a great laugh at his compadres.

Their first obstacle was the Waipi'o River. The water was bone-chilling cold, and in the dark, they stumbled and slipped over the slippery river rocks. George felt every one through his thin tabis. The swift moving river and his heavy backpack made it hard to keep his balance. Pastor Alan, having taken off his sneakers, edged along bare-footed. They thanked God that it wasn't raining and the river wasn't swollen.

On the other side of the river, they hiked to the base of the mountain where the Waimanu trail begins. Pastor Alan peered through the darkness up at what he thought was the craziest thing, a switchback trail zigzagging up the mountain wall at a steep angle. He prayed that God would translate them into Waimanu Valley. *"Lord you did it for Philip in the*

*Bible,*" he pleaded. The Holy Spirit impressed on Pastor Alan that they should stop and have communion right there.

When Pastor Alan had gone to the 'Io Project's North Hawai'i Prayer and Communications Center in Waimea to pick up his communion packages earlier that day, Kahu Strick (Strickland) had three packages ready for him instead of two. Kahu knew that Pastor Alan was assigned only two heiau in Waimanu Valley, but gave him three communion packages. The Holy Spirit knew they would need to do communion at the trailhead. The Holy Spirit also knew the danger Pastor Alan and his team would face on their assignment. Unbeknownst to them, the Holy Spirit had prompted a team of prayer warriors from YWAM to take a trail from Waimea that led to the lookout over the Waipi'o and Waimanu valley areas. The YWAMers arrived at the lookout at 3:30 a.m. to pray for Pastor Alan's team.

Before the three men partook of communion at the trailhead, they repented of their sins and prayed for God's protection. They wanted to be cleansed and covered before taking on not only this physical mountain, but the spiritual one. Communion was a weapon for holiness in an unholy terrain, a declaration in the midst of war. As earthlings attempting to traverse Ta'aroa's lair, holiness demanded that their minds and souls be free from cluttering 'ōpala (rubbish). To proceed with sin would be like warriors who enter a battle without swords or shields, with breastplates broken and helmets defective. They wanted no opening for the Prince of Darkness to attack them. The trail ahead gave ample opportunities for the enemy to kill them.

Whatever the obstacles, Pastor Alan was determined to do it. He knew the spiritual significance of this area. He did not tell anyone but he knew in his spirit that if they did not pull out this spiritual stronghold, Ta'aroa, the evil-smelling squid, would have a hiding place and the final cleansing at 'Iokāne would not be completed. He felt strongly that he had to accomplish his mission by 3:00 p.m. The whole 'Io Project depended on it. He summoned all of his intensity, set his jaw and fixed his heart on the goal. *"Let's Go!"* he said and up the trail he went in the dark at a brisk pace. It was 12:30 a.m. on March 14.

———

*John Kūpuna*
*Hālawa Valley, Moloka'i*

On March 14, in the darkest hour before the dawn, the soul of John Kūpuna wrestled with demons in his night-mare. In his dream, he was praying fervently when the min-ions of Ta'aroa tried one last time to stop him. They were shapeless figures hailing from dark and murky regions of the supernatural, slipping through the realm of dreams, intent on devouring his soul. Taunting him. Binding him. The evil forces were beginning to win against him. His eyes began turning red, his voice changed and became deep. He knew he was being possessed; the demons were beginning to take over his soul! He began fighting with all of his might against them. As he grappled and struggled bound by invisible cords, powerful invisible hands clamping his mouth shut, the name of Jesus would not--could not--be uttered. This name, infused with the power of heaven and earth, was all he needed to overcome the legions of hell. In the dream, he fell on his knees, struggling. Finally, fighting with every fiber of his being, it came from his lips…the whisper of that mag-nificent name…*Jesus.*

As he called upon the name of Jesus, he became stronger and stronger, fighting harder and harder. *"Jesus, Jesus, Jesus!"*

John was now screaming that name. Finally, he broke free of them. Still in the dream he saw that everyone was now dancing, praising God and rejoicing. And then, he awoke. He was free! His alarm clock was ringing. It was March 14, it was time, and John was never more ready for anything in his life.

---

## Kaua'i
## Charmaine

All Charmaine's life she had dreamt of whales. She always dreamt of the same family of whales frolicking in the water. On March 14, she arose at 3:30 a.m. to pray. She was excited; she knew it was a special day for her beloved Hawai'i. Her friend Kathy would be picking her up at 5:30 a.m.

Charmaine began praying for God's grace and blessing over Kaua'i, Hawai'i and her beloved people. Suddenly, the Lord began speaking to her. He asked her to wear something special that day. *"What Lord?"* she replied. She sensed the Holy Spirit leading her to a bag of clothing she was giving away. When she looked inside, there was her old pā'ū hula skirt which had a design of the mountains of Kaua'i. The Lord asked her to wear it. *"Yes, Lord,"* she answered, even though she felt kind of embarrassed. She didn't want to attract attention to herself. When Charmaine prayed again, the Lord asked her to wear a lei. She got up again, found her kukui nut lei and put it on. The presence of her Lord was so strong, she felt as if He was right there with her. She felt like a bride dressing up for her husband on her wedding day. Charmaine went back to prayer. The Lord said, *"Wear a lei po'o."* This is a lei you wear on your head. She opened her eyes and looked up saying, *"But I don't have one, Lord…"* when she spied one on the entertainment center above her. She had forgotten about that one. Charmaine put it on.

When Kathy arrived at her door, Charmaine could see the surprise on her face. Charmaine was all dressed up! They drove to a heiau on a cliff overlooking the ocean where they met the rest of their team. No one could sense even a faint hint of evil. The peace and joy of the Lord, like a cool island breeze on a hot summer's day, infused earth, sky and sea with His love. God beckoned the sun, its rays peered from the ocean's edge, and then radiant fire from that life-giving star filled the earth. In prayer high up on the cliff, they paused to watch the heavens explode with glorious wonders painted by their Creator on the canvas of the heavens, reflecting on the sapphire sea below. Charmaine felt embraced by the presence of her Lord, like she was God's precious bride, the apple of His eye on their wedding day. Then suddenly, whales breached and splashed joyfully on the surface of the sea--the same family of whales she had seen repeatedly in her dreams since childhood! That's when Charmaine realized that her loving and omnipotent God had been watching over her since her youth and had ordained this moment in time, just for her. Here, a memory was born. One where dreams and reality coalesce into beauty, full of wonder, the fragrance of which will remain forever.

When sharing about her experience later, she barely could speak as she choked up with emotion and wept. She said, *"It was like walking into something that was made for us that day. We were made for such a time as this, when we do things God's way. That day, God took apart my heart, he was embracing me. I was in such awe, it cannot be described; it cannot be described!"*

*Pastor Alan Cravalho*
*Waimanu Valley, The Big Island*

George was lagging far behind again; his legs were full of cuts and scrapes from bushes along the trail. George moaned, *"Why did I wear shorts!"* Sometimes he couldn't see or hear Pastor Alan or Delbert as he felt his way along the trail in the dark. With his little flashlight, he could see nothing except the trail right in front of his feet. He had no idea where he was going. Pastor Alan and Delbert spent a lot of time doubling back to check on him. By the time they hiked the 1200 feet to the top of the first ridge, George's face was red and throbbing. He had felt like he started the hike running on only one cylinder and now he was down to one-half! The night was cold but his head was burning. He didn't know if it was his nasal infection or the antibiotics he had taken. He felt dizzy and was out of breath. George kept asking Delbert like a child, *"How much farther?"*

*"Only get 13 more gulches, Cuz."* Delbert said with a smirk. Delbert was not funny! George prayed, *"Help God!"* Three gulches later, George began dropping his packed supplies on the side of the trail. He couldn't carry them anymore. He was lagging way behind the others and could not see or hear them, yet, he felt God's presence. The moon appeared and it became a gorgeous night. He and his friends needed that dim moonlight, it saved them countless times.

Delfin, Ty and Tammy were taking turns praying through the night. At 3:30 a.m. Delfin got up and started praying. At 7:00 a.m., she joined others at the prayer garden on their church site. Some had been praying there since 5:00 a.m. Delfin still felt a twinge of doubt at the spiritual and physical danger her husband was risking because of this project. Was it all real? Then God unveiled a vision to her. She saw in her mind's eye the time they had bought land for a home. They needed to clear the land to build their home and there was an old shack on it. Alan had rented a bulldozer to bulldoze the shack down. She remembered as clear as day the moment the dozer hit the shack. In that exact instant, white rats poured out, scurrying in every direction. She knew that this is what God was accomplishing on this day. The rats' home would be destroyed and they would have to scatter. There would be no place left to hide!

---

### Solid Rock Ministries
### Ka'u District, The Big Island

The team from Solid Rock went back to Ka'u bursting with excitement. One team member awoke at 4:30 a.m. and heard the Lord say, *"Warfare has ended. You are going for such a time as this."* They knew God was with them and felt they were walking out history. They stopped briefly at a store in Waiohinu and heard on the radio that, because of the drought, a huge fire was blazing in the area they needed to enter. The road into that area was closed. This only made the team more excited. They were on the right track; the enemy was angry; but what could he do when the Creator of the Universe was with them? They got into the car to leave but it wouldn't start. They just got more excited, prayed fervently, tried again, and the car started right up. As they approached the area of the fire, there were police and road blocks everywhere. They just smiled and waved at the police and drove around the road blocks! No one stopped them. At the first two heiau(s), the Spirit of God suddenly fell upon them in such power that they began to weep uncontrollably. One woman heard hundreds of crying children and another saw the bodies of ancient sacrifices. One tough Hawaiian man shared, *"You know, I rarely cry. It's a macho thing I guess, but I just broke down and wept. It wasn't us, it was supernatural, all of the men broke down and wept."*

The kūpuna who had helped them find the heiau(s) met the team at the gate to the third heiau. They had never shared with her what they wanted to do there. She was not a Christian, how would she take it? When they shared with her about it, this tough old kūpuna began to weep and thank them for allowing her to be a part of this historic time. She shared that Kaʻu was in such a horrible drought that the cattle were dying. At the heiau, they had a glorious time of prayer and repentance with God and their new friend.

---

## Solid Rock Ministries
## Kona District, The Big Island

Before dawn, the team from Solid Rock Ministries assembled in a Kailua-Kona parking lot where the human sacrifice heiau once stood. This was the area recently identified by the *West Hawaiʻi Today* newspaper as Kailua town's worst area for drug dealing. But now it stood empty. Just as the first rays of morning sun drive away the darkness, so on this morning those controlled by the forces of darkness had slinked away like so many shadows. Although the heiau was gone physically, the curse of the blood spilt upon this land remained. The team walked around the area of the former heiau, each member praying as the Lord led them.

They all were drawn to the same spot. In the words of Dee, one of the team members, *"We all seemed to end up in this one spot and we began praying there. Then some really eerie stuff began happening. There was a really strong smell of fresh blood coming from that spot and then we heard people weeping. It was the first time I ever experienced something like that!"* The team repented for what their ancestors had done there, had communion, and in Jesus name, declared that the sin on the land had been forgiven. Then they commanded the spiritual minions of Ta'aroa to leave. They had no more claim to the land there and must go in Jesus' name! The curse upon the land that gave them the right to remain there was broken! As they were commanding the demonic forces to leave, all of a sudden, all of the dogs in the area began to howl. Their hair stood on end as the mournful wailing of the dogs continued. They all felt a chill as the spirits of darkness left the area. The dogs stopped howling just as suddenly, and then there was peace.

---

### Nāpo'opo'o, The Big Island

A team of five women were responsible for three heiau(s) in Nāpo'opo'o. At one heiau near the ocean, they couldn't walk around it on the ocean side to pray because of huge crashing waves. Yet, they felt God was saying they needed to walk around the entire perimeter of the heiau. They joined hands in a circle and began to pray fervently. As they were praying, the roaring of the waves began to fade. When they finally opened their eyes, there were no waves! They just looked at each other, smiled, and walked around the heiau. Reports from others along the Kona Coast said the waves never stopped crashing that whole morning.

---

### Island Breeze
### Ahu'ena Heiau in Kona, The Big Island

Ahu'ena heiau sits on a peninsula of land that curves around a small sandy bay called Kamakahonu, in front of the King Kamehameha Hotel. This small sandy bay is a part of the larger Kailua Bay that fronts Kailua town. From the heiau grounds there is a panoramic view of the Kona coastline. Far off, you can see Kealakekua Bay, the *Way of God* Bay, where Captain Cook landed and where Henry ʻŌpūkahaʻia, a young Hawaiian boy, left for New England. It was he who later inspired the first missionaries to come to Hawaiʻi. A short distance across Kailua Bay, you can see Mokuʻaikaua, the first church established by the missionaries in 1820, the present church having been built in 1835. Across the street from the church is Huliheʻe Palace. It was at one time the residence of Princess Ruth Keʻelikōlani, who was an ancestor of Daniel's hānai family, the Eatons. Directly in front of the heiau across Kamakahonu Bay is the Kailua pier. Under the pier still remains the "Plymouth Rock of Kona" that the kahuna nui Hewahewa prophesied the New God would land upon. On that very rock, the first missionaries had landed in 1820, fulfilling many Hawaiian prophecies of the return of the True God of the Hawaiian people. It was an area filled with history!

In proper Polynesian protocol, Kealoha, the kahu for Island Breeze, chanted their entry onto the heiau grounds. In their group were people from Samoa, Tonga, New Zealand and Hawaiʻi, all performers at the lūʻau show. The realization of the importance of what they were doing made them tread softly. There seemed to be a holy hush over the area; the presence of the Lord was so powerful, it permeated the grounds. The team repented for the sins of their ancestors, the spilling of innocent blood in that place, and partook of communion. God then spoke, *"I am calling the warriors of Polynesia to rise up and come forth!"* He was calling especially the men to rise up, not as physical warriors this time, but as warriors of ʻIo; warriors of light, life, pono (righteousness), and aloha! God was calling forth warriors who would have the courage to stand for what is pono and protect the weak. A man from New Zealand leapt up and began a fierce Maori haka (war dance). Eyes blazing with holy fire, he declared the death and resurrection of Christ and the victory of Christ over the devil. The air sizzled with the power and glory of God.

God spoke to them again, *"What was stolen from the Polynesian people by Pā'ao will be returned and a deep desire within these island people to know Me will be released."*

Paoakalani, the kumu hula (hula master) of Island Breeze, who bore an uncanny resemblance to her ancestor, Queen Emma, ended their time by dancing a hula to "Ke Alaula." Ke Alaula is one of the most beautiful and popular songs in Hawai'i which speaks of a flaming pathway of light opening up the generations. They wept with joy as they realized that this was being accomplished this very day.

---

### Pastor 'Tex' Texeira
### Kona, The Big Island

Pastor Tex and his wife Shelly were at their assigned heiau on Kailua Bay. From their vantage point, they could see all the way down the Kona coast. They had not yet heard of how God quieted the waves at one heiau farther down the coast. The waves were crashing all along the west coast of the Big Island that day. Over the sound of the crashing waves, they could hear Island Breeze at the King Kamehameha Hotel, praying, chanting and doing the haka at Ahu'ena Heiau, the next heiau on the coast from where they were. Shelly began hearing the cries of people and began to weep. They prayed, asked God to forgive the sins perpetrated on that ground, and partook of communion. All of a sudden, both of them sensed at the same time that it was done. At that instant, a giant wave like no other crashed onto the shore and then receded so far, that Tex thought a tsunami was coming. Then the water returned to normal. It was done!

Now Tex and Shelly could look forward to ʻIokāne. They soon would be picking up Daniel and Landa at the Kona airport, then driving them out to North Kohala. What amazing things would God do at the cleansing of that last heiau!

---

## The Summit of Mauna Kea

Beth and Tim Murph and their team of twelve stood on the summit of Mauna Kea. Mauna Kea is not only the highest place in the islands but the highest mountain in the world if measured from where it rises up from the ocean floor. It is also the only place in Hawaiʻi where snow falls regularly in the winter. People would go surfing in Hilo in 78° water and then go snowboarding on the same day just for the unique experience.

Although the team drove nearly to the summit, it was still difficult to hike the rest of the way in the thin air. But Beth was riding on the clouds! The day had finally arrived when she would fulfill what the Lord called them to Hawaiʻi eight years ago to do—go to the summit of Mauna Kea and pray over her beloved Hawaiʻi.

The view was magnificent; the hearts of the people were expectant; and the presence of the Lord was overwhelming. The Lord had asked Tim the day before to go to each moku (ancient Hawaiian district—larger than an ahupuaʻa) on the Big Island and take a vial of soil from each one. In obedience Tim had spent all day driving around the island to each of the six districts. In each district, God guided him to take this road or that and told him where to stop and get the soil or sand. In each area the Lord led him to he came upon a hidden altar or place of worship that was not listed in any books they had read or reported by any kūpuna they interviewed.

Tim took the vials of earth from each district and poured them onto the ground there atop Mauna Kea. They prayed and wept over each district, crying out to God over the different problems each one had, including the long drought in Ka'u and Kohala. The team then shared communion and poured part of the wine on the soil from the six districts and placed a piece of communion bread there. They knew it was because Iesū shed his blood for them that the sin of leaving the true God could be forgiven. This sin had resulted in the sacrifice of thousands of innocent Hawaiians to other gods, now the land could be cleansed of this evil stain.

Wayne Santos, a well known Hawaiian musician and worship leader on the Big Island, heard the Lord say, "*I am the Lord of these islands even though people don't know it yet.*" They then stood and proclaimed over the Hawaiian Islands healing and freedom because of the sacrifice of the Lamb of God, Iesū Kristo! 'Io, through the shed blood of his Son, was again Lord of these islands! The Lord's words inspired Wayne to write a song about this historic day that would forever be stamped in their memories.[1]

When they had arrived on the summit of Mauna Kea, they couldn't see Hilo because it was covered in thick clouds. As they prayed and worshipped God, they witnessed an amazing occurrence. The thick clouds began to be sucked out of Hilo as if by a giant vacuum cleaner. The clouds were being sucked through the "saddle," the mountain plateau between Mauna Kea and Mauna Loa. The clouds streamed out in a line past Kona towards the Southwest Pacific.

Now, with a panoramic view in every direction spread out before them, they felt as if they truly were on top of the world! Beth was ecstatic. She could see in her mind's eye, the golden pearls of oil dropping upon the land from the hem of the Lord's garment. As they continued singing praises to God, they heard a heavenly choir join in the rejoicing.

As they headed off for ʻIokāne, everyone wondered what would happen when the final heiau was cleansed!

---

## Kahu John Trusdell
## Wahaʻula, The Big Island

Kahu John, a direct descendant of Hewahewa and Pāʻao, decided to take responsibility for Wahaʻula Heiau, the first human sacrifice heiau built in Hawaiʻi by Pāʻao. Wahaʻula was located near the ocean below the active Kīlauea volcano. There it remained in the midst of vast lava fields for around 800 years but finally was overrun with lava just seven months before on August 12, 1997. The team felt that God went before them to clear the way. All they had to do now was walk out this next step of cleansing.

After a long and difficult drive in the dark, Kahu John's team arrived at the end of the rugged, four-wheel drive road that had been bulldozed through the lava fields. Kahu checked his watch as they began their hike over the newest lava fields. It was 4:30 in the morning and still dark. The team moved cautiously. Hiking over the sharp, uneven lava is tough even in daylight. Fresh lava has a thin glassy layer on top of it that can cut up your shoes in no time. In the sun it glistens with shades of blue-green and gold, but this glassy layer is fragile and dangerous. It cracks off when people walk over it and is sharper than glass. Another danger of fresh lava is that a thin hardened crust can hide a cave-like lava tube underneath. Many people have fallen into lava tubes and been hurt or killed. In some places, the tubes are large enough to drive a tractor trailer through. In areas with an active lava flow, such tubes can carry a river of molten lava. Kahu John stepped on a lava "bubble" and the lava crumbled away beneath his foot. Somehow, he did not fall in. It was not deep but he knew a fall like that could cut a person to shreds.

Because the heiau was now covered by an ocean of solid rock, they weren't sure they could find it. There were miles and miles of black lava fields as far as they could see. Since 1983, more than 550 acres of new land had been added to the Big Island. This does not count the thousands of acres of land covered by earlier flows. Many people had gotten lost in this vast lava wasteland. Landmarks here are forever changing, with each new lava flow causing a settling and shifting of lava ledges. The team hiked for quite a while, looking for landmarks; they knew they were close because the lava was getting really fresh. It was then that Kahu's brother, Del, said, "Uhh, John, I think we better stop. I think my slippahs (flip flops) are melting."

At that moment, they turned toward the ocean and saw a welcome sight. Although lava had covered the heiau, a long pole marking the heiau site was still sticking out from it. They had arrived at the heiau just as the sun was rising. The glorious Spirit of their God swept over them on that barren lava field and they all spontaneously began to weep. As the rays of the sun began dispelling the darkness above them, they looked toward the ocean as an awe-inspiring sight unfolded before them. Framing the red and gold rays of the sun, were two colossal columns of smoke rising straight up into the clouds on either side of them. They had passed directly over a lava tube through which molten lava flowed to the ocean. When the searing liquid rock poured into the cool ocean, it exploded into shards of black glass and hot steam. The crashing waves would eventually smooth the black shards of glass and a new black sand beach would be born. Another river of lava poured out of its tube on the far side of them, thus creating the two massive pillars of smoke before them.

It reminded them of the Lord's presence that Israel must have felt as Moses led them through the desert of Sinai, being a pillar of smoke before them during the day and a pillar of fire by night. In this otherworldly setting, standing in the midst of a vast frozen ocean of black lava, titanic pillars of smoke framing the rays of the morning sun, tears streamed down their faces. In His majesty, God was cleansing all of the innocent blood with fire—His fire! Tears streaking his face, Kahu John turned his gaze toward the heavens and petitioned God to forgive the sin of his ancestor Pāʻao and cleanse the stain of innocent blood from the land. The team solemnly partook of communion and poured the wine on the ground which began to steam. April Trusdell danced a hula of praise to her God on the frozen ocean of lava. They remained there awhile, drinking in the presence of the Lord and their wondrous surroundings. It was an experience they would never forget! Kahu John now gazed northward, wondering what wonders God had in store for them at ʻIokāne.

---

*Pastor Alan Cravalho*
*Waimanu Valley, The Big Island*

Pastor Alan slipped on a kukui nut and landed flat on his back with his legs flailing up in the air. Good thing it was not when the trail was on the cliff! Pastor Alan was sore and embarrassed but he did not stop. He knew if he stopped, he wouldn't make it. And Delbert, looking at the hefty pastor said, *"I ain't going carry you out!"*

The trail was in poor condition and it had been difficult hiking at night. Still, they thanked God for the moonlight and that it was not raining. At least the streams were not swollen and easy to cross. The further they hiked the worse the trail became. At times the trail descended at a 58-62 degree decline, like the hands on a clock dial if one hand was at the "5" and the other at the "55." The trail was washed out in areas and covered in others with landslides and boulders. It was also covered at times by slippery leaves hiding kukui nuts that were like round marbles under their feet. Sometimes, when the trail was very steep, all of them slipped and fell on loose rocks or slippery leaves and kukui nuts. They would slide down before gaining a grip on a root or rock to prevent themselves from gaining momentum and careening out of control down the steep trail or flying off of the cliff. In the dim moonlight the trail glowed with an eerie light while the gulches in the shadows were pitch black. If they slipped off the trail it looked like they would slide into endless darkness. Like with a child, Pastor Alan and Delbert kept encouraging George. *"George, just a little more. George, almost there! Just a few more ridges, George!"*

Having hiked eight grueling miles of precarious switch-back trails up and down mountain ridges, Pastor Alan, George and Delbert were finally nearing the last obstacle, the perilous 1200 foot cliff down into Waimanu Valley.

---

*Kahu Mau*
*Hāna, Maui*

At 4:30 in the morning, Kahu Mau's team was already gathering in the parking lot below their assigned heiau. Suddenly, a bright light flashed across the northwestern sky.

They decided to stop and have a time of prayer. As they were praising God, a cross appeared in the clouds with the full moon shining behind it. It was unbelievably beautiful!

Kahu Mau said later, "*We had been ready for an epic struggle with the principality of the islands but instead found the peace and love of the Lord overwhelming us. We later found out that every team experienced the same thing.*"

As Kahu Mau's team climbed up to the heiau, seven women intercessors prayed fervently at the bottom of the hill. It was then that Kahu Mau saw the gigantic Hawaiian warrior standing on the wall of the heiau to oppose them. But suddenly, the giant warrior turned and fled. Kahu Mau wheeled around and was staggered. He saw with open spiritual eyes, the chariots of God flying in, flooding the morning sky above them! At the same moment, all seven intercessors saw the same vision in the sky, what looked like a magnificent white horse flying in!

---

### East Maui

The team of Kaulana Correa, George Kaimiola, Jill and Tia Tahauri and Jacob Mau covered three heiau(s) on the undeveloped east side of 10,000-foot Haleakalā Crater. This team consisted entirely of Hawaiians except for Tia, who was Tahitian.

At one heiau, whose name meant "Great Tahiti," they prepared to enter with prayer. As they blew the conch shell, a brilliant sun rose out of the Pacific Ocean, its golden rays streaking the morning sky. Thus prepared, they entered solemnly and cautiously. They sensed a murderous spirit in the heiau, the spirit of Taʻaroa, the giant heʻe (squid). From his head at Taputapuatea his tentacles stretched out across the

Polynesian triangle. The East Maui team prayed to oki or cut the tentacle that reached from Tahiti to the heiau. Suddenly, they saw a vision of the cut-off tentacle retracting back to Tahiti. With unity born of many months of praying together, these intercessors moved like a well-oiled machine, receiving visions, scriptures, and words of knowledge confirming what to do next. Never before did God open their eyes to see so clearly in spiritual realms.

Tia located the sacrificial stone. Kaulana, being descended from ali'i, stepped forward. She knew what atrocities her ancestors had committed at this place. Thousands of innocent Hawaiians had been brutally murdered because of a system designed to benefit her ancestors. As Kaulana, filled with remorse, tentatively approached the stone, she began to tremble. About six feet from the stone, she began to weep and shake uncontrollably. Her spirit groaned in pain. Kaulana could barely stand as her body began to convulse violently. She cried out in a loud voice, *"Father, it hurts!"* The pain her Lord felt over all of the innocent Hawaiian lives lost was pouring forth from the Holy Spirit within her. She didn't know if she could survive the pain! She couldn't take another step. In agony she fell to her knees and then onto her face, wailing in uncontrollable anguish over the horror that occurred on that very spot.

Then the Lord opened their spiritual eyes and unveiled to the other team members visions of the violent horrors that occurred at the heiau and of the innocent blood crying out from the earth. Tia had a vision of great streams of blood rolling down the stone into the earth, from sacrifices of ten men at a time. Jacob saw the victims being laid on their back facing the mountains and a Mū crushing their heads with a large stone.

They were all weeping and wailing uncontrollably as the Lord revealed to them vision after vision of horror.

They finally gathered enough strength to take communion and repent of all the sins of their ancestors and ask God to heal their land. They looked up at the hills and saw a vision of people standing on the hills, mothers, daughters, sisters, wives, fathers, brothers, and sons in helpless agony. They couldn't see the brutal horrors occurring in the heiau but they could hear the tortured screams. Helplessness pervaded them and their eyes were deadened. The team prayed that God would heal that wound in their people; that forgiveness of sins committed generations ago would ripple into this generation. Then they saw a vision of a cross appear over the stone. Jesus in his glory also appeared, radiating mercy and grace. Innocent blood came pouring out of his body, permeating the stone and seeping into the soil. The team wept at the price paid by their Savior so their sins could be forgiven and their land healed. They knew it was done. The blood of Jesus—poured out in sacrifice—had cleansed the land.

*Akea Eaton*
*West Maui*

The Lord told Akea to be at the remote Honokōhau Valley in West Maui at daybreak. When he was growing up, he was always told, *"Don't go to the heiau; bad things happen if you have no purpose there."* But Akea knew well his purpose there that day.

The night before, Akea was so excited he couldn't sleep. It was like the night before a championship football game. He kept checking the clock and praying. Finally, at 3:30 a.m., he was happy to get out of bed and go for it. The Lord said to him, *"This is the most important day of your life."* Akea knew it was a make-or-break day in the history of his people.

Akea had three other men with him on his team, tough guys, most of whom he had known from "small kid time" (childhood). He loved these men; they were all warriors. If there were any three guys he wanted to go to war with, these were the three. Akea was about 250 pounds and one of his other friends was 350; they made their way to the heiau like defensive linemen. The two smaller men were jumping through the brush like running backs in their excitement for the battle. When they all arrived at the heiau, however, the Holy Spirit suddenly filled them and all these tough guys fell to their knees weeping uncontrollably in repentance for the murders their ancestors perpetrated there. These men cried so long and hard that their eyes were swollen from weeping for their people.

Honokōhau Valley rose up into the West Maui Mountains ending in 'Eke Crater at the top. 'Eke Crater was a place of witchcraft that is also the watershed of West Maui. Hawaiian tradition says that it used to be an altar to 'Io but was defiled by Pā'ao. The tradition says that Pā'ao hid his idols in 'Eke Crater.[2] The polluted water now flowed into all of West Maui, bringing a curse upon the land. After weeping until their eyes had no more tears, they partook of communion. God told them *"Right here,"* this was the spot of sacrifice. They poured the rest of the communion wine on that spot. They heard God say, *"Well done!"*

The Lord then told Akea, *"Look up."* With open spiritual eyes, he saw that an enormous angel that dwarfed 'Eke Crater was now looking over it towards Moloka'i. They then turned to pray toward Hālawa Valley in Moloka'i where Daniel and Landa were. Little did they know that at the same time, Daniel and Landa were praying towards Maui. The Lord spoke again, *"Pray and war!"* They prayed until Akea saw the mighty angel stand up over 'Eke Crater and stretch over Honokōhau

Valley to plant his other foot on the mountain above Hālawa Valley right on the tentacle line. Suddenly, a shaft of light appeared on the Hālawa Mountains at the exact moment the angel stamped his foot down. Immediately everything broke open in the Spirit as the floodgates of heaven burst open! The four men broke into rejoicing. Never were their eyes and ears so open to see and hear in spiritual realms!

Akea reported, *"There was such peace as we went, we knew it wasn't us, God had gone before us. We are so blessed that God chose us for such a time as this. No one will get glory out of this except God!"*

Akea and his team felt led to ʻIao Valley, one of the most sacred places in Hawaiʻi. They knew that ʻIao was another name for ʻIo. The valley had been desecrated by bloodshed. Many battles had been waged over this sacred place and during one major battle, the ʻIao river was dammed up by bodies of the dead and the water ran red with blood. God spoke to them, *"Listen to the land; it has something to tell you."* Then it seemed like the land began to cry out to them because of the bloodshed. It seemed as if that the land was in pain wanting desperately to be free of the curse imposed upon it by the sins of men. It reminded them of Romans 8:19-22, *"All of creation waits with eager longing for God to reveal his children. *[20]*For creation was condemned to lose its purpose, not of its own will, but because God willed it to be so. Yet there was the hope *[21]*that creation itself would one day be set free from its slavery to decay and would share the glorious freedom of the children of God. *[22]*For we know that up to the present time all of creation groans with pain, like the pain of childbirth"* (TEV).

They took communion again and shared it with the land, pouring the wine on it and planting the bread in it. God spoke, *"Listen to the land again!"* Then it seemed the land said it was set free from all of the bloodshed. They prayed wherever the

Lord directed them. They prayed at a burned-out Hawaiian meeting house, at an overgrown area farther up the valley and at former taro patches choked with weeds.

Akea and his team returned home exhausted. It had been a long and glorious day that they would never forget. They basked in the afterglow of the Lord's presence but prayed fervently at 3:00 p.m. because Daniel said to. Daniel didn't say why, he just said to pray because it was very important.

---

### Daniel and Landa
### Hālawa Mountains, Molokaʻi

At 5:30 a.m. Saturday, March 14, Daniel and Landa were strapped into a small "bubble" helicopter flying from Maui to pick up Zennie Sawyer at the Molokaʻi airport. Daniel was sitting in the co-pilot's seat watching Jacob Mau's friend, Mike, expertly maneuver the helicopter. Through the clear plastic bubble that curved to just in front of his feet, Daniel could see in the pre-dawn light, the gray ocean tinged with orange racing below him. The sky was clear when they started from Maui, but by the time they picked up Zennie and flew out towards the Hālawa mountain ridge, ominous dark clouds surrounded them. Mike buzzed up and down the steep ridges looking for a place to land. It was windy and foggy. It seemed to Daniel that he could see only 20 to 30 feet in front of him; but they were flying so fast, he could not be sure. If they had not known that the Lord had called them for this, they would have been in stark fear.

The treetops seemed to be zipping past just below Daniel's feet. As he gripped his seat he thought, "*If a really tall tree suddenly appears in front of us, Mike will have his eighth crash!*" Sometimes Mike would soar over a sheer cliff face. The sea cliffs of Moloka'i are said to be the highest in the world at around 3,000 feet. Unexpectedly they would find themselves hurtling out into space with thousands of feet of open sky below them, the clouds far below.

Searching everywhere, Mike could not find a place to land. *"I will try one more pass!"* he shouted to his three passengers. Daniel, Landa and Zennie started praying fervently. It was then that Mike spotted a tiny open area between Ōhi'a trees on a narrow ridge. Watching his tail to make sure it was free of the trees and fighting the strong wind that blew across the top of the narrow ridge, he landed on a precarious spot about the size of a queen-size bed! Any other pilot would have refused to land in those conditions; it was only because of his great expertise and his desire to fulfill Jacob's wishes that Mike attempted the landing at all. Over the roar of the 'copter, Mike told Daniel, *"The wind is too strong! If I stay here on this narrow ridge the helicopter is in danger of being blown over. I'll fly down to the valley to wait. I'll be back for you in an hour."* As Mike roared off, the three found themselves alone on a misty mountain top. Mike had set his GPS to the spot, but because of the thick mist, none of them knew where they were.

It seemed that as soon as Mike roared off, the winds died down and everything became still. Daniel had lamented before they left that they had no one to lead worship, but when they got to the mountain top, rare Hawaiian birds were singing beautiful praises to their Creator. Joining the song of the birds was a sound they thought must be made by crickets. Later Zennie learned the sounds came from rare Hawaiian Kāhuli snails, an endangered species. None of them had ever heard the Kāhuli before. God had provided the most rare and exquisite worship for them. This misty wonderland was the purest of pristine sites. Few, if any, humans had walked upon its wet and spongy ground. The air felt heavy with moisture and dew collected on their faces. Landa recalled, "*It was as if the mist was the hand of God caressing our faces.*" They were experiencing Romans 1:20 firsthand, "*For since the creation of the world His invisible attributes—His eternal power and divine nature—have been understood and observed by what He made, so that people are without excuse*" (ISV).

The little team had been ready for an epic struggle with the fearsome Lord of Polynesia but instead found the peace and love of God overwhelming them. There was no opposition, the minions of Ta'aroa fled before the King of Kings and Lord of Lords! They hiked down a narrow deer trail about 50 yards and came upon the exact spot the Lord had revealed to Landa in a vision, a spot with a tall dead tree. In near zero visibility, Mike had landed only 50 yards from the spot God had shown her! They consecrated the summit to 'Io, dedicating the land to the True Lord of Hawai'i. They petitioned God to forgive the shedding of so much innocent blood in worship to other gods in the valley below them. They poured the communion wine upon the earth and prayed that the cleansing blood that Jesus shed on the cross for the sins of man would seep down into the bowels of Moloka'i and raise up Moloka'i to be what God intended it to be. They prayed that what God deposited in Moloka'i would rise to the heights and spread as a blessing to the world. The wine would eventually seep down into the watershed and permeate Hālawa Valley from top to bottom. Water of Life would flow from this mountain!

The presence of the Lord was overwhelming; they immersed themselves in it. They could picture what eternity would be like, basking in the presence of God forever! It was like God was singing a love song to them and they were singing back to him. It was the Song of Solomon, the love song of the King looking for his precious bride and his bride longing to be wrapped in her husband's presence. They desired to remain as long as they could in the intimate embrace of their Creator in his pristine creation. Zennie was overwhelmed by the experience and, not wanting to lose any of the details, later tried to journal her feelings. However, her experience could not be put into words. Then the thought came to her to put it into a song. The poetry, feelings and spiritual sensations began to flow forth effortlessly and capture the essence of the experience.[3]

It was so natural to worship God when one was immersed in that majestic throne room of glory He had arranged just for them! At the end of their time, they faced east towards Hālawa Valley and began proclaiming its freedom from the tentacles of the Evil One and its return to the One True God. Immediately, a hole appeared in the dark clouds and the morning sun streamed through it upon them. They basked in the golden warmth of the sunshine. It seemed as if God's pleasure was being poured out upon them. The surrounding mists were gilded in gold.

Little did they know that Mike had already made several passes through wind and rain searching for them. Mike later told Jacob that while down in the valley, he grew concerned he might not be able to find them. Even with GPS, the mountains were now shrouded in dark clouds, and it was windy and rainy. The little team had also moved away from the spot he landed on. He had flown back and forth several times hunting for them and was beginning to despair that he had lost them. It was then that he saw the brilliant light. He headed towards that light, flew over the ridge, and found the little team kneeling in a clearing, that heavenly light shining down upon them like a giant spotlight!

They learned only later that Akea was standing on Maui at the next heiau on the major tentacle through the islands at the exact same moment praying towards them. From Maui,

Akea had seen the beam of light appear on the mountains above Hālawa Valley just as the majestic angel planted his foot down on it!

Mike landed easily in the clearing to retrieve them and as the helicopter rose back up into the morning sky above Hālawa Valley, the clouds seemed to give way before them, the bright morning sun now burning the mist away. It was only later that they realized it was rainy and windy everywhere except wherever they were! It would have seemed impossible to them at another time, but not that day! It was miraculous but, somehow, not surprising at all to them, not when enveloped in the presence of an Omnipotent God! How glorious it was being embraced in the bosom of the Creator in that sacred place! They were aglow with their experience as the 'copter zipped back to Maui for their flight to Kona on the Big Island and 'Iokāne. They passed directly over a mother humpback whale and her calf. As Daniel watched the whales slip out of view beneath his feet, he thought of Moki's "whale trials" and their soon coming time at 'Iokāne. What surprises would the Creator have in store for them there!

---

*Pastor Alan Cravalho*
*Waimanu Valley, The Big Island*

Pastor Alan, George and Delbert were finally climbing down the last 1200 foot ridge into Waimanu Valley. This was the most treacherous ridge. Sometimes, this steep trail was only a narrow 12 to 18 inches as it angled down the ridge. At times it slanted down at a steep angle and also towards the edge of the cliff sideways! George was climbing this steep trail in tabis meant for flat reefs! The trail was in bad shape and they had to climb over washed out areas, slippery leaves and landslides while clinging onto little roots and shrubs to avoid, what was at times, a sheer drop of hundreds of feet to the valley below. Because the trail slanted towards the edge, one slip on these could mean death. Less determined hikers might have deemed the trail impassable and turned back but turning back was not an option for these men.

Except for a little piece of communion cracker, George had hiked nearly nine grueling miles up and down gulches and ridges on empty. He was past exhaustion. Lightheaded and weak, he edged along the narrow and slippery ledge clinging onto little roots and shrubs on the cliff wall. It seemed like his heavy backpack was trying to pull his upper body away from the cliff wall he was feebly clinging onto and hurl him over backwards down the cliff. It was daylight now but George didn't know if that was good or bad. Now he could *see* how far he might fall!

It was so steep coming down that Pastor Alan's toes scrunched hard against the front of his sneakers with each step. The jarring on his knees and shins from climbing up and down 12 mountain ridges and 13 gulches was now causing shooting pains up his legs. But Pastor Alan kept trudging forward, one step after another. And then it happened: he gazed up from his shuffling feet and realized he had reached the valley floor. He had at last arrived in Waimanu Valley!

---

*O'ahu*
*Honolulu*

The team of six people assigned to upper Honolulu was searching for its heiau. It was on private land, but they weren't sure where. After one failed search, they prayed again for guidance. The team felt led to another gate leading to a private area. The Lord gave them a word of knowledge that this was the one.

As the team drove up, a man was driving out of the gate. They asked him where the heiau was. He informed them that it was on the property inside of the gate but that special arrangements, permissions, and approval by the Board of Directors were all needed before access to the site could be granted. They would not be able to get in that day.

But as the man left, for some reason, he told them to ask at the maintenance shop behind them. When they arrived at the shop, they discovered that the regular foreman was not working that day. His replacement, a young Hawaiian man, didn't know what to do with the group so he called the manager's office. The manager just happened to be out that day, too. The phone rang and rang, and then, because there was no answer, the call was automatically transferred to the office desk clerk. The office clerk repeated to them that permission was granted by submitting a letter for approval to the Board of Directors ahead of time. However, because this group was already there and there was no one else the clerk could ask what to do with this group; she left the decision of what to do with them to the weekend maintenance foreman! Meanwhile, the team had been sharing with this young Hawaiian man what they were there to do. When he heard their reasons for wanting to go to the heiau, he not only offered to escort them, but provided them with three golf carts to ride in. They went rejoicing all the way. If the Lord of the Universe wants something done, it will be done, and first class! Upon arrival at the heiau, they chanted an oli before entering in and then prayerfully entered. The team prayed upon the heiau, thanking God for his gracious forgiveness for the many innocent people murdered there. Then they prayed for a blessing upon the Hawaiian people and the land. The presence of God shining upon their faces, they rode away in their golf carts the blessed children of the King of Kings!

## Wai'anae

The team that went to Wai'anae and Makaha was led by Kahu Hanohano, a man who had experienced firsthand the powerful forces at work at the heiau(s). He said he would never have taken on this task if he did not know God wanted it. His team of Hawaiians had scouted one site ahead of time but could not find the heiau because of thick brush covering the entire area. They returned this day to the same area, having prayed in faith that God would show them the way. They did not realize that, just before March 14, there had been a huge fire in the drought-stricken area. When they arrived that day, the heiau stood out as clear as day. All of the brush was burned away! As they began to pray, one of the Hawaiian men could hear people crying. After half an hour of praying, he saw a whirlwind and smoke rise out of the heiau. He thought the place was still burning and went to take a closer look; the whirlwind rose right out of the ground and went straight up into the air. It was an awesome, supernatural sight!

---

## Kailua

Pastors Rick Frazer and Gary Langly led a team to their assigned heiau in Kailua, O'ahu. They arrived at 9:00 a.m. to find a Hawaiian civic group cleaning up the heiau grounds. Following proper Hawaiian protocol, they approached the group leader, introduced themselves, shared the reason they were there, and asked for permission to come onto the grounds. Permission was granted, and the leader of this group gave them a guided tour of the heiau. They learned that the heiau was one of the first three heiau(s) built on O'ahu and was originally dedicated to 'Io.

*Many years later, Pā'ao* seized control of the heiau and turned it into a place of human sacrifice. There were several springs at the heiau site used to wash the bodies of the sacrifice victims. One Hawaiian woman in the group had felt led to bring a calabash with Hawaiian salt (evaporated sea salt) in it. Another received from God a word from 2 Kings 2:20-21 (KJV): *"And he said, bring me a new [bowl], and put salt therein. And they brought [it] to him. And he went forth unto the spring of the waters, and cast the salt in there, and said, 'Thus saith the* LORD, *I have healed these waters; there shall not be from thence any more death or barren [land].'"* They threw the Hawaiian salt into the springs, then prayed and proclaimed the waters healed. They felt the glory of God wash over them. The team sensed that things were being released from the ground and heard the cries of innocent people whose blood had been shed there. It seemed that the land, after waiting so long, gave a long sigh of relief.

At the end of their time at the heiau, the team thanked the Hawaiian Civic Club and asked if they might pray for them. They all stopped their work, joined hands with the group and prayed together that God would bless the Hawaiian people, the work of the people there, their heritage and the land.

---

## Pastor Alan Cravalho
### Waimanu Valley, The Big Island

Pastor Alan stood facing the ocean near the right wall of the valley. *"Lord, help me find this heiau!"* he pleaded. The only information he had about its location was an archeological survey from 1896. It said the heiau was along the south wall. A landslide had covered much of the south side and he wondered, *"Is it under the slide? God you didn't bring us all this way to not find it!"*

George was so exhausted and in such pain, he just wanted to lie down and die. He did not want to move, ever. He watched Pastor Alan and Delbert tramping back and forth, scouring the brush for the heiau. He felt sick, exhausted, scratched up and discouraged. *"These guys are nuts!"* he thought. As Delbert passed by, George questioned where they needed to go next on this crazy journey. Delbert pointed to a far ridge across the valley and said, *"See that cliff? We have to climb up it and then climb down the rope suspended from the cliff into that gully behind it."* George's look was of pure despair, *"How did I ever get roped into this crazy mission!"*

Pastor Alan was saying he couldn't find the heiau. George just started praying, *"Oh, God, I am too tired to go all over this stupid valley looking for a broken down heiau in the shrubs."* That's when they realized it, George was sitting on it! He was on the ocean side edge of the platform! Pastor Alan moved the grass and vines behind George and saw the flat surface and smooth stones of the platform. The landslide had covered the middle of it. They would have never known it was there if George had not sat on it. George was pleased, *"Well, I did my part!"*

They prayed at this heiau and sensed such a peace about this place that they would have never known it was a place of human sacrifice.

Pastor Alan pleaded, *"Lord you need to show us where the next heiau is ASAP. Time is going to run out. It took us six hours to get in* (a very fast time) *and we are hurting now, it may take us eight or nine hours to get out!"*

They crossed the Waimanu River on another rocky bed of river rocks. The archeological report said the next heiau was in the middle of the valley near the beach. When Pastor Alan had obtained the hiking permit, he was told that the trail across Waimanu Valley was approximately one and a half to two mile long. Pastor Alan was trying to judge where the middle of the valley was. He prayed again for help. He couldn't imagine walking back and forth across the many acres of the middle of the valley hunting for a heiau hidden under the brush. He was much too exhausted for that! Pastor Alan plunged ahead and ran smack into a swarm of bees. He stepped back a few feet and, as the bees cleared, he beheld an incredible sight. "He had walked right up onto an area paved with smooth stones. The tsunami of 1946 had wiped this entire region clear of any ancient structures but could this be the floor of the heiau? God confirmed that he should pray here. The little team took communion and Pastor Alan poured oil around the area. It seemed as if God's presence flooded the whole valley as they prayed.

"Okay now," said Pastor Alan, a man still on a mission. "I am going back to the first heiau and pour oil around it, too." George could not believe Pastor Alan had the energy to do that. He was looking in terror at the cliff Delbert said they would have to climb by rope.

Delbert motioned to George, saying, "Let's head back."

"I thought you said the next one is down da rope into da cliff!"

"Oh, Dat! I was just kidding, bra."

George glared at Delbert with a real Hawaiian "stink eye." Delbert was not a funny man. "Bra, jes wait! You goin' get it!"

---

O'ahu
Kahu Dean Spencer
Papakōlea

Kahu Dean Spencer was supposed to rise at 6:00 a.m. on the morning of March 14, but he didn't want to go. At 7:00 a.m., he heard the Lord say like a Hawaiian father, "You better *go, boy."* So he reluctantly arose and, still with a heavy burden, went with his wife, Robin, to Punchbowl Crater. They prayed and had communion at several places within the crater. The Lord had told him to save part of the communion wine to throw into the waters off of Kewalo Basin. So he took the remainder of the wine down to the bay in obedience to God, not understanding why he was doing it. When he got to the basin, still carrying a heavy burden, he walked out to the farthest point and threw the wine into the waters as the Lord had instructed him. Immediately, Dean felt the burden he was carrying lift off of him. He was amazed but still didn't understand what happened.

It was the next week before the Lord gave him understanding through Exodus 7:20, *"And Moses and Aaron did so, as the Lord commanded; and he lifted up the rod, and smote the waters…in the sight of Pharaoh, and in the sight of his servants; and all the waters that [were] in the river were turned to blood. And the fish that [were] in the river died; and the river stank, and the Egyptians could not drink of the water of the river; and there was blood throughout all the land of Egypt. And the magicians of Egypt did so with their enchantments: and Pharaoh's heart was hardened, neither did he hearken unto them; as the Lord had said."* (KJV) And the Lord spoke to Dean's heart, *"As innocent blood caused death and hardness of heart, the innocent blood of My Son, sacrificed for you, will bring life and softened hearts."*

---

*John Kūpuna*
*Hālawa Valley, Moloka'i*

John Kūpuna and his team had been assigned seven major luakini heiau(s) in Hālawa Valley; more luakini heiau(s) were concentrated in this valley than in any other area in Hawaiʻi. In the old days, Molokaʻi was the most feared place in Hawaiʻi. It was the crossroads of the main tentacles coming from the northern Hawaiian islands of Kauaʻi and Oʻahu and the Southern islands of Hawaiʻi (the Big Island) and Maui. Molokaʻi had 17 human sacrifice heiau(s) whereas Lanaʻi, an island nearly the same size as Molokaʻi, had only one!

As John Kūpuna led his team up the valley, he petitioned God to break the strongholds of his enemy one by one. In the spirit, he saw the light of God piercing the darkness. As the blood of human sacrifice was cleansed, the Oppressor's minions retreated.

John most wanted to get to the kahuna training heiau far up on the corner point of Hālawa Valley. When one stood on the platform of that heiau, a spectacular ocean panorama was revealed. One could look back into the valley to the kukui grove and see the heiau next in the tentacle line behind it and also follow the line of the tentacle out over the ocean in the other direction to Honokōhau, Maui.

Because he came from a kahuna ʻanāʻanā line in Hālawa Valley, John couldn't wait to break this one! His warrior blood was fired up, and he was keen to confront the powers of darkness and set himself and his family free from the curse of murder and innocent blood!

As John climbed up onto the platform of the kahuna training heiau, a gale-like wind swept across it from the sea. He shouted into the wind, "*Father! We repent for the sins committed here, the sins of our forefathers. We proclaim the blood of Christ that was shed to cleanse sins and break the curse over this valley!*" John found himself screaming, ordering the demonic forces to leave in the name of Jesus. "*You have no more right! You must leave NOW because Jesus commands it. Jesus sets us FREE!*" The whole team began to war with him.

Suddenly John sensed something break in the spiritual realm and great peace and freedom flooded into his soul. He knew he was finally set free from the curses and demons of his family's past! On that wind-swept platform, perched high over Hālawa Valley the team began spontaneously singing, no, they were victoriously shouting:

*"Our God is an awesome God*
*He reigns from Heaven above*
*With wisdom, power and love*
*Our God is an awesome God!"*
—chorus from the Rich Mullins song "Awesome God"

It was indescribably glorious!

---

### Moloka'i from the air

Flying back to the Big Island, a Hawaiian woman named Nettie was disappointed. She wanted so badly to be a part of the cleansing of her beloved islands. She had prepared diligently for it and then she found out that her son was to win an award at Kamehameha School on O'ahu that same day. She was torn but knew she had to be there with her family. She prayed that whole day for the people who were going out to the heiau(s).

On the way back from O'ahu, she was still saddened that she couldn't take part, yet she knew she did the right thing to be with her son. Casting a glance out of the airplane window, Nettie saw Moloka'i below her. She thought, *"That is where Daniel and his team went today."* Then she saw it, a gigantic, magnificent triple rainbow arching over Moloka'i! She couldn't believe it. In Hawai'i, there are a lot of rainbows.

There are even many double rainbows, but in all her life she had never seen a triple rainbow like she was seeing now. Was it some kind of trick of the sun upon her window? Just then she heard the passenger in the seat in front of her say, *"Do you see what I am seeing?"*

*"You mean you see it, too?"*

Yes, it was real. Nettie knew it was a sign. The rainbow represented the promise and blessing of God. It was the Father, Son and Holy Spirit blessing the prayer that day. Her Lord had blessed Nettie to be a part of it after all. She thanked God that He had placed her in the perfect spot to witness this once-in-a-lifetime phenomenon.

---

## Pastor Alan Cravalho
## Waimanu Valley

Feeling the peace of God flooding Waimanu Valley and the main purpose of their mission accomplished, Pastor Alan, George and Delbert decided they could finally break their fast before attempting the long and arduous hike out. Fasting had definitely increased the physical dangers of the hike but the physical danger was not their primary concern; it was the spiritual one. They had brought the staple food of the locals, spam musubi; which is a fried piece of spam on a rectangle of sticky rice wrapped in seaweed. Not the best food to break a 6 day fast! However, they gratefully gobbled this down with chicken wings. They ate more than they should have after a long fast and now really didn't want to move! They sat there looking up at the cliff and felt like immovable pieces of lead.

Being a scenic valley, several tour helicopters flew into Waimanu while they were eating. The three men dragged themselves up and desperately tried to wave down the helicopters yelling "*RESCUE AHHHS! RESCUE AHHHS!*" They were serious; this was an emergency! They were completely spent and couldn't imagine hiking all the way back! The helicopters didn't pick them up; they probably thought the three waving men were drunk. They should have let George lie on the ground like he was dead. Acting dead would have been easy for him!

They laughed about how silly they looked. It is a good thing they still had their Hawaiian, "Hang Loose," sense of humor about them; if they had taken their ridiculous situation seriously they would have just sat down and cried. Finally, knowing they needed to finish their mission, they dragged themselves up. Feet like lead, they lurched towards the cliff.

Climbing up the steep 1200 foot ridge out of Waimanu Valley, Pastor Alan was still praying, "*God, okay, I am ready, anytime I am ready to be translated. Beam me up!*" He was fatigued beyond reason but refused to even dwell for a second on his pain or how tired he was. If he did, he knew he wouldn't be able to survive.

Pastor Alan kept focusing and kept hiking, placing one foot in front of the other one ridge and one gulch at a time. Even Delbert, as experienced and strong as he was, started coming down the ridges with sticks like ski poles to support his weary legs.

The food George ate finally kicked in and gave him the energy he needed to continue. Now that the sun was out, he could see what was over the edge of the trail he had climbed in darkness. Over the trail edges that he couldn't see before were sheer drops down to river rocks far below or into stands of hala trees with leaves like serrated knives. Looking at these, George really knew his Lord had watched over him. An amateur hiker, he had hiked past these on an uneven and slippery trail in the dim moonlight while carrying a heavy pack that shifted each time he slipped. He was also out of shape and exhausted, weak and lightheaded from fasting, sick and dizzy from a nasal infection, and had only a few hours of sleep in the last two days. Considering all of this, one could easily understand how dangerous this trail had been for him. Hiking in, George had felt nearly delirious, hiking in a dreamy state, not knowing what he was doing or where he was going. He couldn't remember much of the hike; it was just a blur of pain.

Near the halfway point of the trail back, Delbert and George took a much needed break to remove their shoes and stick their aching feet into a mountain stream. Pastor Alan didn't join them. He knew if he stopped he wouldn't be able to get up again. His old softball injuries were acting up and his legs were locking up. Delbert and George watched the hefty pastor trudge on, laughing at him because his stiff, short steps made him look like Frankenstein. And yet, they were in awe of his determination.

Pastor Alan had felt pain shooting up his legs when he arrived in Waimanu Valley. Now, after hiking back four miles up and down six mountain ridges the pain was mind-numbing. If he thought about still having over four miles, six more ridges and seven more gulches, to go, he would have lost it! Instead he kept focusing to just put one foot in front of the other.

Delbert and George wanted to rest a while longer, but they had to get back to Waipi'o and get a message to Pastor Strick (Strickland) in the North Hawai'i Prayer and Communications Center before their mission was pau (finished). They reluctantly and painfully dragged themselves up and limped after him.

# 24
# 'Iokane Heiau

*"There is a casting off, I am casting thee off. Do not come in to possess me again; let me not be a seat for thee again! Let me not know thee again; do thou not know me again. Go and seek some other medium for thyself in another home. Let it not be me, not at all! I am wearied of thee--I am terrified with thee! I am expelling thee. Go ever to the Vai-tu-po (River-in-darkness), into the presence of Ta'aroa, thy father, Ta'aroa, the father of all gods. Return not again to me. Behold the family, they are stricken with sickness; thou art taking them, thou art a terrible man-devouring god."*

—Tahitian Chant for the Casting Out of a "God"

It was early afternoon on March 14, 1998. Daniel and Landa flew into Kona airport where they were picked up by Pastor Tex and Shelly for the trip to 'Iokāne. After their experience on Moloka'i, they were flying high emotionally. Daniel looked up at the clear blue sky, the warmth of the sun streaming down upon him, and felt blessed to be a Child of God. They drove the hour and a half to North Kohala sharing about the experiences of the day. Before they knew it, they had arrived at the end of the road. There were many cars parked there already. As they hiked in, they began meeting people who excitedly related what had happened that day. Moke arrived and he and Daniel began to organize the excited and growing crowd. Word had spread about what was to transpire at 'Iokāne and there were more people than they expected. Kawika Kahiapo and Leon Siu, the other founders of Aloha Ke Akua, had flown in from O'ahu for this historic event. Zennie had flown in from Moloka'i. Tim and Beth Murph and their team had driven down from Mauna Kea. There were people from all over the Big Island!

Moke designated those who would go up to the heiau; these were 'Iokāne relatives, close friends and those who would be involved in what 'Io had told Moke to do.

Moke was scanning the crowd for the fourth man whom 'Io had told him must enter the heiau to be a part of the cleansing, the one whose face he couldn't see. While he was standing next to Daniel, Moke pointed to a man and said, *"You da guy!"* The man he picked was Kahu John Trusdell. What Moke did not know at the time was that Kahu John was a descendant of Hewahewa, the last high priest over the Kapu System and a direct descendant of Pā'ao. It would be years later that Kahu John, while talking with his kūpuna, found out that he also had 'Iokāne blood! Daniel was the only person God chose to be a part of the cleansing who was not related by blood to Moke's family.

Now Moke had his team, and those going to the heiau began the hike up. As they approached the heiau, a somber quiet fell over the group. The air was electric with anticipation. As they neared the "outer court" of the heiau, Moke instructed them to remove their shoes. A hush had fallen over the 'āina. Even the birds seemed to be still. Moke looked around and, although he had never been there before, he found the landmarks he had seen in his vision. He asked the family members to pray in the outer court and, as 'Io had instructed him earlier, he placed a man at each corner of the heiau outside of the walls. At the first corner was a conch shell blower, at the next, a shofar (Hebrew ram's horn) blower, and then a conch blower and at the last corner, a shofar blower. They were instructed to blow all together when the heiau was cleansed. Moke did not realize it at the time, but he had picked people of many ethnic groups to blow the victory triumph. He did not realize that this event would have significance not only for the Hawaiian people, but for all nations on earth.

'Io had told Moke that the heiau would be cleansed by the shed blood of his Son, Iesū. The four men would cleanse the heiau on the inside by "standing in the gap" and repenting for the brutal murder of thousands of innocent Hawaiians at that very place. They would then partake of communion and pour the communion wine, "Christ's blood," onto the altar, the four walls and the corners of the inside of the heiau. Then they would go outside and pour the wine on the four outside walls and corners.

When Daniel and Landa had started out to 'Iokāne from Kona several hours before, they departed under a brilliant sun and azure skies that stretched from horizon to horizon. They were so focused they did not notice the encroaching darkness in Kohala until Daniel was about to enter the heiau. He was wondering why it seemed so dark. He looked up and stared at the sky in amazement.

'Iokāne heiau is situated on the Kohala Mountains on the north side of the Big Island. Looking towards the ocean from the heiau, a magnificent panoramic view greets you. One can see all the way to the horizon to the left and to the right where the ocean meets the sky. Across the sea in front, one can see the island of Maui floating in the distance. If you turned and look behind, you could see the majestic Kohala Mountains rising up into the clouds. Somehow, thick dark clouds had stealthily rolled in blanketing the entire expanse of the sky! Not one speck of open sky remained! The dark clouds brooded eerily; like death lingering in the air, suffocating the light of the sun. The clouds were so heavy and thick it had become dark, even though it was mid-afternoon. It looked like dusk, just before nightfall, the daylight being suffused by an evil twilight that cast a strange, foreboding pall on the land.

On any other day, Daniel might have felt fear and apprehension at this ominous "miracle," but not on this day. Not when you were walking in the presence of the Almighty! Daniel thought in stunned amazement, *"Where did all these clouds come from and how did they get here so quickly? There were only a few white fluffy clouds when we arrived at the airport just a few hours ago!"* It was as if the giant evil-smelling squid, Ta'aroa, shot out a black cloud of ink over Hawai'i in a desperate attempt to hide himself and survive.

Missionary Richie Lambeth had witnessed the clouds rolling in from the beginning. He stated in his report that, *"As I left Kona, it was sunny with a gentle breeze blowing in off the ocean. The blue skies were a perfect complement to the garment of praise that I felt wrapped around my shoulders. Everything seemed light and easy until I made the turn through Kawaihae and started out on the road to Kohala. Almost instantly the winds began to whip up, and I noticed that ominous dark clouds began to sweep down from Mauna Kea and Mauna Loa. I felt apprehensive at once and immediately began to pray. My praying felt sluggish and difficult at best. I did not feel freedom in the spirit. Then my apprehension magnified as I noticed that the same kind of dark clouds were sweeping in from the ocean as well. I was stunned by this supernatural occurrence--the ominous movement of clouds blowing from opposite directions towards Kohala! Warfare raged in invisible realms; defensive tactics in the heavens created the black, suffocating cloud of smoke roiling in from an unseen fire. I knew that Satan was bringing in a cover of spiritual darkness to combat our last offensive of truth and righteousness at 'Iokāne.*

*"Then another wonder unfolded before my very eyes as if by the order of a demon general. The clouds began to separate slightly and took on the form of shields. Each shield looked to be about 10 feet long and 5 feet wide. Then all at once all the shields came together and the sky was completely blanketed and the sun was totally blacked out. I shuddered. I have been in Hawai'i for 40 years and I have never seen anything like that. I knew then that this battle had more spiritual significance than any of us had imagined. Satan's army was aligned in the sky in full battle array and they were exerting every bit of spiritual energy they had to prevent what was about to happen."*

Supernatural armies in full battle array were facing off in the heavens for a titanic final struggle for supremacy over Hawai'i. An epic battle loomed ahead.

It was nearly 3:00 p.m. and about 175 people had gathered at 'Iokāne to pray and witness the event. There were quite a few kūpuna(s), descendants of ali'i(s), pastors and missionaries, the Island Breeze leadership team and several kumu hula (hula masters) were among the many people there. Most were at the bottom of the mountain trail, some were outside of the heiau and the four men were preparing to enter 'Iokāne. Daniel looked at the other three men and knew they were feeling the same way he was, humbled and thankful that God would choose them to walk out this historic moment! His body vibrated with excitement and anticipation, he had never felt more alive; and yet, it felt like a dream!

As Moke signaled the three men to follow him, he stepped reverently into the heiau entrance. It was such a holy and historic moment, the men seemed to be walking in a surreal dream state, they sensed a vibrating or buzzing in the spirit realm. As the four men stepped forward into the inner court of 'Iokāne, the weight of the sin of the brutal murder of thousands of innocent Hawaiians in that place became overwhelming. The burden became so heavy they could no longer stand; they fell on their knees in the center of the heiau. A supernatural grief welled up from the depths of their na'au (belly/soul) and came pouring forth. They wept uncontrollably; moved by the supernatural sorrow of the Holy Spirit within them. The four men wept so hard over the thousands of innocent Hawaiian lives lost there that their tears falling on the dry dirt made a circle of mud under their bowed heads.

The communion they took there was unlike any communion they had ever taken before. Words cannot explain the reverence and thankfulness they felt for what Jesus had done for them and for Hawai'i. Man was made in God's image and was sacred to Him. 'Io had given orders that man was not to be killed. They were trembling with an overwhelming humility and thankfulness at the love of God, that He, in his marvelous mercy and grace, would forgive and wipe away the sin of the murder of many thousands of His beloved Hawaiian children and heal their land. They poured part of the communion wine onto the mud of their tears and then buried part of the communion bread in that earth of tears and communion wine of which Jesus said, *"This is my blood...which is shed for you."*

---

### Pastor Alan

Pastor Alan kept pressing on, determined to get a message to Pastor Strick that their mission was finished. They finally crossed the last river, and limped to their truck in Waipi'o Valley moaning and "ouching" all the way. They were

so exhausted they could barely climb into the truck. They
were laughing at each other as they moaned and groaned,
trying to pull themselves in. Even Delbert's legs were hurting badly. He was yelping "Ouch! Oww, Oww!" every time
he had to shift gears. George was yelling at Delbert to avoid
the bumps and potholes in the road; each one Delbert hit
made George yelp in pain. At 5 minutes to 3:00 p.m., after
a six-day fast, being awake 30-plus hours and having hiked
a grueling 18-plus miles, Pastor Alan finally reached a pay
phone at the "Last Chance" store in Kukuihaele.

When Kahu Strick answered, Pastor Alan said just one
sentence: *"The targets have been disarmed, the enemy has been
scattered."*

---

Just before 3:00 p.m., Nalani, the North Hawai'i coordinator, was in prayer at the bottom of the trail leading to
'Iokāne heiau. Suddenly, she felt an urgency to call Kahu
Strick. They were still praying for Pastor Alan, wondering if
he had finished his assignment. She asked her friend Clarisse
if she had any bars on her cell phone. *"I have one dot."* She
said, *"I will try to call Pastor Strick."* Clarisse prayed fervently,
called and got through! Kahu Strick said, *"Praise God! I had
just asked God to have someone call me. Pastor Alan just called,
mission accomplished!"* Clarisse's phone went dead. She tried
to call back several times but could not connect again. The
phone connected just long enough for her to hear those
words.

---

Landa was just telling Zennie, *"I sense that there has been
a breakthrough."* She wheeled around to see Nalani walking
towards her. *"Mission accomplished!"* Nalani reported, *"Pastor*

*Alan just called. They did it!"* Then it happened. That's when the sky split open.

———

After partaking of communion, according to 'Io's instructions, Moke, Daniel, Kahu Gaymond and Kahu John anointed the altar and the four corners and walls inside of the heiau with the wine of the communion. Then, they came out and began anointing the corners and walls outside of the heiau. As Daniel poured the communion wine on the last corner, the shofar blower at that corner suddenly pointed towards the sky and screamed in excitement, *"Look up! Look up!"* Daniel looked up and was staggered! The sight was so strange that it took several seconds to register that he was not dreaming or seeing a vision. He blinked his eyes several times and thought, *"I can't believe it! It...it is real! It is really happening!"*

Right above him, a flaming pathway of golden light streaked across the black sky as far as he could see; light streamed down upon the land and ocean. The moment he had poured the communion wine onto the last corner of the heiau, the light had streamed down upon 'Iokāne. The brilliant path of light stretched back over the Kohala mountains as far as he could see in line with Mauna Kea and Waha'ula and forward in the other direction streaking over the ocean to Maui, across the body of Maui, across the top of Haleakalā, and as far as he could see right in line with Honokōhau on the head of Maui and Hālawa Valley on Moloka'i. God's dazzling pathway of light illuminated precisely where the main gripping tentacle of Ta'aroa once stretched across the islands! The massive blanket of dark clouds had been sliced down the middle by a perfectly straight line of light from horizon to horizon!

At the same time, the people far below at the bottom of the trail suddenly saw a path of radiant light streak across the sky, streaming light down upon the heiau; they realized instantly that the work at the heiau had been accomplished.

Kahu Kawika Kahiapo was hiking up to the heiau when it happened. He said he was looking down because it was dark and the trail was rough. Suddenly, it seemed like a light was turned on over his path. When he looked up, he saw a path of light on the ground before him going up the Kohala Mountains as far he could see and when he turned around, it extended down the trail and across the sea behind him all the way to Maui. He said later, *"It was like living in a dream."*

Leon Siu was standing on the outer wall of the heiau looking towards the Kohala Mountains. He saw what looked like a curtain of brilliant light from the clouds to the ground being drawn in a straight line down the mountain. It came right towards him and the heiau, streaming the glorious light down onto them as it zipped by. Leon reported, *"It was amazing how bright the curtain of light was, it was as if the noon day sun was directly above the clouds."* It seemed to Daniel like a special effect in a Moses movie! John McCollum, who was at the bottom of the mountain trail when it happened, said the clouds zipped open like a hot knife through butter.

Richie Lambeth reported, *"The clouds appeared to be like thousands of shields welded together, and I wondered as we prayed, what would become of them."*

*Then one of the most incredible things I have ever seen in my whole life happened. Right exactly above us a section of the shields split and the blinding radiance of the sun shone through them in power. It raced all the way to the ground right in the midst of us and it seemed like the gleaming rays bounced off the ground and saturated everyone there. The Glory of the Lord was definitely among us and our worship went to a new level.*

*Then something even more incredible happened. The shields continued to divide section by section as if seared apart by a giant laser in the heavens. The heavenly laser continued to slice a flaming path through the clouds heading out across the ocean. I was amazed as I watched this sign in the heavens as a 100-foot path of brilliant light split the shields apart and what seemed to be the full power of the noonday sun raced down to dance across the water. As the intense sunlight hit the ocean, millions of dazzling light rays would explode across its face. It was one of the most glorious experiences I have ever had!"*

Those who saw the path of light splitting the blanket of clouds from the beginning say it took between 10 and 30 seconds to zip across the heavens from the Kohala Mountains, across the ocean, and over Maui as far as they could see. It was difficult to judge the time it took when one was in stunned awe and there was pandemonium breaking out all around. The veil of darkness, the domination over Hawaiʻi of the Lord of Darkness, Taʻaroa, was rent in two. The curse was broken! The heiau now belonged again to ʻIo through the sacrifice of Iesū Kristo, his Son.

The prayer warriors who were at the bottom of the trail came up the mountain rejoicing in wonderment, every face at ʻIokāne shining as if having looked into the face of God. The people humbled themselves together before God in the outer court of ʻIokāne and took communion all together. In the meantime, the pathway of light took on the shape of a twisting tentacle and then straightened out again. It grew wider and wider. To Daniel it seemed that the thick blanketing clouds were rolling back like two giant scrolls. If so many people had not seen it, they would think it was a dream. No one had ever experienced anything even remotely like this!

Richie's report continues, *"The rest of the sky for as far as I could see was still covered with that ominous blanket of dark* clouds until the pathway of light reached the horizon. Then wonder upon wonder happened, for as soon as the path of light reached the horizon the light began to break through the shields on both sides. It actually seemed like the shields were exploding and before I knew it, the clouds were completely gone and the sky was clear for as far as the eye could see. I have never seen the sky more blue or the sun more radiant. The heavens were declaring that they were the handiwork of God and the Glory of the Lord reached down and kissed the earth and all of its inhabitants. I was overwhelmed by the manifest presence of the Lord and I wept with gratitude at being alive at such a time as this and being given the honor of witnessing the Lord reveal Himself as the Captain of the armies of heaven!"

## Pastor Alan

As Pastor Alan hung up the phone and the three men hobbled back to the truck, Delbert put a weary hand on pastor Alan's shoulder and said, "Pastor, this is the bottom line... YOU'RE A BULL!" Pastor Alan looked at Delbert and said, "Look at me. Delbert, look at me!" Delbert was so tired he could barely lift his head up to look at Pastor Alan. "I cannot take one iota of credit, this was a miracle. This is a testimony of the incredible grace and mercy of God. This is God and God alone, for His Glory."

Spontaneous praise and rejoicing flowed at 'Iokāne like sweet wine and the celebration began in earnest. God's presence and His pleasure at this pivotal event in Hawaiian history was completely indescribable! Moke shared with the gathered crowd how God had brought so many Jonah examples to him to get him there. At the exact moment he was sharing about how he had been running from the Lord like Jonah, a huge whale breached high out of the sea right behind him! To everyone's delight, the God who commands the universe was again confirming Moke with his omnipotent sense of humor. With an overflowing joy, they prayed in Hawaiian, sang and chanted God's praises in Hawaiian and danced the hula and haka in worship of their God. For the first time, without one iota of shame or insecurity they worshipped God fully as Hawaiians, with all their minds, hearts, souls and might. They did this in a freedom and joy they never experienced before. They finally realized that God not only accepted their Hawaiian praises, He loved and coveted them! God had desired this day much longer than they had! On this glorious day, God had joined their split Hawaiian souls together. The Hawaiian half and the Christian half joined together fully and seamlessly as one for the first time. For the first time in their lives, they felt fully loved by God as they were—Hawaiian! The people worshipped and praised God until the beautiful Hawaiian sun set over the ocean under clear skies. As the last edge of the sun dipped beneath the ocean, a whale breached right over it, a fitting supernatural ending to a supernatural day.

God, 'Io, Jehovah, had not forgotten or forsaken his native Hawaiian children. He had lovingly led them from the beginning to this place He had chosen for them and had dwelt with them and cared for them ever since. Even when they left Him, He never abandoned them, preserving a remnant of those who would follow him for the sake of the whole people. He sent prophets to confirm his word and his aloha for them. And finally, He restored His original legacy of aloha to His Hawaiian children through a Christian descendant of the true priestly line of 'Io, by the blood of His Son, Iesū. The last high priest of the Hawaiian "Old Testament," Moke, turned over the priesthood of 'Iokāne heiau to the Great High Priest of the Hawaiian "New Testament," Iesū Kristo, the Son of 'Io.

The sky turned dark at 3:00 in the afternoon on that fateful day 2000 years ago when the Son of God shed His blood and died on the cross at Calvary to cleanse all creation from the curse of sin. As the thick heavy curtain in the temple of Jerusalem on that day ripped in two from top to bottom, opening free access into the most holy place of the Jews, so the thick dark sky ripped in two over the most holy place of the Hawaiians. "Ke Alaula," the flaming path of light, pierced the darkness, opening up the generations again to their True God, 'Io, through His Son, Iesū.

The Old Testament of God's legacy to the Hawaiian people and the New Testament of his Son, Iesū Kristo, joined seamlessly together as one. The True God of the Hawaiian people would be no longer perceived as a foreign God calling them to a foreign religion; He was their God, He was 'Io, the God of Aloha, calling his children HOME!

After 800 years, The Prophecy of The One—fulfilled!

# 25
# Epilogue—
# After The 'Io Project

*"When I shut up heaven and there is no rain, or command
the locusts to devour the land, or send pestilence among My
people, $^{14}$if My people who are called by My name will humble
themselves, and pray and seek My face, and turn from their
wicked ways, then I will hear from heaven, and will forgive their
sin and heal their land. $^{15}$Now My eyes will be open and My
ears attentive to prayer made in this place. $^{16}$For now I have
chosen and sanctified this house, that My name may be there
forever; and My eyes and My heart will be there perpetually."*

—2 Chronicles 7:13-16 KJV

As the people left 'Iokāne and began to drive home, a gentle rain began to fall. By that night, people all over the
Hawaiian Islands were reporting that the rain was pouring
down.

## Kona

After they left 'Iokāne, one team went to the pu'u (hill)
on the Kona coast where they prayed regularly. They saw a
haze, like a fog coming over the mountains from the east. But
it was not a normal haze or fog because it was shining and

243

bright. They asked each other. *"Do you see that?"* It was like the Lord was confirming the day. The old strongholds were broken and his presence was moving in.

God gave one of them a scripture, Ezekiel 43: 4-9 (KJV), *"And the glory of the* LORD *came into the house by the way of the gate whose prospect [is] toward the east. So the spirit took me up, and brought me into the inner court; and, behold, the glory of the* LORD *filled the house. And I heard [Him] speaking unto me out of the house; and the man stood by me. And He said unto me, Son of man, the place of my throne, and the place of the soles of my feet, where I will dwell in the midst of the children of Israel for ever, and my holy name, shall the house of Israel no more defile, [neither] they, nor their kings, by their whoredom, nor by the carcasses of their kings in their high places. In their setting of their threshold by my thresholds, and their post by my posts, and the wall between me and them, they have even defiled my holy name by their abominations that they have committed: wherefore I have consumed them in mine anger. Now let them put away their whoredom, and the carcasses of their kings, far from me, and I will dwell in the midst of them for ever."*

---

### John Kūpuna
### Hālawa Valley, Molokaʻi

John Kūpuna was driving his family friend, Loke, home from their time of prayer in Hālawa Valley. They were praising God and basking in the afterglow of the day. They saw a man hitchhiking on the side of the road and stopped. He was not going their way, but John introduced himself. *"Hi Bra, I'm John."* Loke also introduced herself. And then the man looked in between them and waited. Finally he inquired, "*Who is that sitting in the middle?*" John and Loke looked at each other, there was no one there! The man kept looking between them. Finally John said, "*It's the Holy Ghost!*" The man looked confused and backed off as they drove away laughing and praising God.

John Kūpuna is still the kahu of his family church on Moloka'i.

---

## Maui

Kahu Joe Tabuya, Jacob Mau, George Kaimiola and people from other teams drove to the top of Haleakalā, the House of the Sun, the tallest mountain on Maui to thank God for the day and proclaim God's glory. They prayed that the "Sun of Righteousness" would shine upon Maui. "*Behold, the day cometh, that shall burn as an oven; and all the proud, yea, and all that do wickedly, shall be stubble: and the day that cometh shall burn them up, saith the LORD of hosts, that it shall leave them neither root nor branch. ²But unto you that fear my name shall the Sun of Righteousness arise with healing in his wings; and ye shall go forth, and grow up as calves of the stall. ³And ye shall tread down the wicked; for they shall be ashes under the soles of your feet in the day that I shall do this, saith the LORD of hosts*" (Malachi 4:1-3 KJV).

Kahu Joe couldn't believe his eyes as a pure white whirlwind appeared as if to say, "*It is done!*"

All of the Maui leadership of the 'Io Project are still serving the Lord. Akea is now a kahu. Daniel and Akea are still close and get together whenever they can.

---

## Pastor "Tex" Texeira

It wasn't until he was leaving 'Iokāne that Pastor Tex realized the gauge on his gas-guzzling '55 Chevy was below empty. The car got about eight miles to the gallon and when it was below empty, he knew he had about four miles to get to a gas station. He turned east along the coast to go to Hāwī to fill gas, even though it was in the opposite direction from where he was going. Unfortunately, the two gas stations in the sleepy little town of Hāwī were already closed down for the day. What should he do? He certainly wasn't going to leave his baby, the cherried out '55 Chevy, on the side of the road. Tex and Shelly prayed and decided that God was with them all day, He could be with them a little longer. They decided to try to make it to the gas station in Kawaihae about 20 miles away. Miraculously, they made it there! They were thanking God when they saw that the station in Kawaihae was closed, too! There is a 24-hour gas station there now but there wasn't one in '98. They thought, *"Well, God got us this far, let's go for the Royal Waikoloa to see if that station is open."* Miraculously, they made it there! Pastor Tex estimates he got 35 miles on a half gallon of gas.

In the month after March 14, Pastor Tex's church grew by 30 percent. They were mostly Polynesians. He had always focused on bringing, as he would say it, "Mokes, Titas, and Blalas" to the Lord. Basically, this meant Polynesian bullies, drug dealers, gang members, and overall tough guys and gals. The guys that were now walking into church were the worst of the worst, guys even Tex would be afraid to talk to. Guys that were former drug dealers and brawlers in his church dropped their jaws when they saw them walk in. These were bad dudes. They would walk into church with their common-law wives of 15 years and all their kids and ask to be married.

Tex would say, "*This is only the beginning, but when God kick-starts your car, you'd better put the pedal to the metal or it can die out. We need to go for it full blast now!*"

---

## Pastor Alan Cravalho

Pastor Alan, George and Delbert looked like soldiers who had just returned home from a war and, indeed, they were in a war! That night George's legs were so battered they were locking up and cramping. When he got home, Tammy had to help him out of the truck while he "ouched" and groaned. George wanted to just lie down on the bed but couldn't even get his legs high enough to get onto it. Tammy had to lift his legs one by one onto the bed. He didn't know how he would do worship for Sunday service the next morning. He was a ball of pain from head to toe. But Sunday morning came and both he and Pastor Alan awoke feeling great, as if nothing had happened the day before. Neither of them could believe it. It was as if they never hiked those grueling 18 miles into Waimanu Valley and back!

It was only after the 'Io Project that the Lord told Alan why he had to hike in. He needed to walk and pray the whole long and painful trail of tears into Waimanu Valley to redeem every step that the sacrifice victims and their mourning families walked to the heiau(s) in Waimanu Valley. It was God who closed the door on the helicopter and the zodiac boat. It was God who cancelled that transaction, not man.

In August of 1998, Pastor Alan, George, Delbert and many from their church walked the 51 miles from Hilo Harbor to the Hawaiian Homes Office in Waimea, covering the Hāmākua coast, the area God told Pastor Alan to steward. Each step of the way they prayed that God would move and bless that land.

On the grounds of the King's Chapel Honoka'a property, Pastor Alan built a prayer garden and prayer center (which was birthed out of the 'Io Project) and a radio station. For over nine years Pastor Alan had worked diligently and persevered in prayer faithfully through many trials and setbacks; finally he had nearly finished their beautiful new church building. Now he could just settle into his beautiful new facility and the easy life of the pastor of an established church. However, that is not Pastor Alan. God called him to start a new church on the Hilo end of the Hāmākua coast. So, without any hesitation or regret, he turned the keys of the beautiful new building he labored and prayed nine years for, over to a new pastor. What a dream for any new pastor! Pastor Alan joyfully started a new church all over again, from scratch, without land, building or funds on the Hilo side of Hāmākua.

Because of his proven faithfulness his senior Pastor, Dr. James Marocco, now has asked Pastor Alan to become the District Pastor over the Kahului District on Maui. The King's Cathedral church in Kahului has an average Sunday attendance of several thousand people. Pastor Alan has been given the responsibility to care for some 800 families in the Kahului area. He has also been given the leadership roll in their Ethnic Ministries division which includes their Filipino, Marshallese, and Spanish ministries. In addition to this, he has been designated as the Construction Projects Coordinator for the ever expanding King's Cathedral church and school. Dr. Marocco gave him this job because of his proven ability to start difficult projects from nothing and see them through to their completion. Pastor Alan continues to oversee the Honoka'a and North Hilo churches that he planted on the Big Island.

Pastor Alan is being sought after to speak at other churches more and more often. However, when he is at his home church, you will still find him praying for Hawai'i and the world every morning from 5:30–6:30 a.m. seven days a week at the King's Cathedral Kahului Prayer Center.

George and Tammy returned to Maui in 1999 to raise their new son who was born on their 18th anniversary. He is their child of prophecy and remembrance of March 14, 1998. George owns a music studio and is a sound engineer, producer and songwriter. George says he still has in his heart to write a song about his Waimanu experience, but it needs to be in God's right time. We are still waiting to see what a song about their experience would sound like!

## Aloha Ke Akua

Because of the breakthroughs experienced by Aloha Ke Akua in Hawai'i, other indigenous peoples are asking for their assistance. Aloha Ke Akua is now a worldwide ministry which continues its work of breaking the cords that bind indigenous people from Christ. The ministry has expanded to the point that each of the three founders, Leon Siu, Kawika Kahiapo and Daniel Kikawa now have their own ministries. They still do projects together under the banner of Aloha Ke Akua, support each other in their individual ministries, and meet together regularly.

Beth and Tim Murph are still involved with Aloha Ke Akua and are praying for their next major assignment from God. They feel that it is coming soon.

Moke and Pali 'Iokane are taking an increasing role in the ministry of Aloha Ke Akua and also have begun their own ministry. They have a gifting for worship and are writing many wonderful songs inspired by 'Io and Iesū Kristo.

———

Daniel has written two more books, produced two films, two music CDs, and completed many other projects for Aloha Ke Akua since the 'Io Project. He has also finished his Ph.D. in Intercultural Studies. His materials are now being used in missiology classes around the world, and he has taught at missionary schools and Bible seminaries on every continent on the subject of culture and the Gospel. God is leading Daniel and Landa more and more into Asia.

Daniel is also continuing to follow God's instructions to *"Tell all people that I have this same story of love and faithfulness for them, too."* With this in mind, Daniel wrote the script and was the lead producer for a film called "God's Fingerprints in Japan." The film's purpose was to break the three cords over a new people group, the Japanese. To break the first cord, God told Daniel the same thing He did in Hawai'i: tell the Japanese people that the Creator God of the Bible is the same Creator God of Japan. The Japanese Creator God is called "Amenominakanushi," meaning "The God in the Glorious Center of Heaven."

An interesting thing happened after the film was distributed. A family of two generations of pastors watched the film. This family is descended from one of the founding families of Japan. Their ancestors were the priests of the first emperors of Japan. By the amazing providence of God, they became the possessors of a rare genealogy scroll that goes back for over 2000 years of their ancestors to the founding of Japanese society and then continues on to a mythical period. When they watched the film, the Holy Spirit spoke to the matriarch of the family. She saw the name of Amenominakanushi and thought, *"Could this be the same name that is at the top of our family genealogy scroll?"* The Holy Spirit then told her it was important that she look at the family scroll. They had not looked at it for a long time and as Christians, were not really interested in it. It was when they looked at it that they found the name of Amenominakanushi at the top of their scroll followed by a creation account similar to that in the Bible!

This is tremendously important because God is saying that He wants his Japanese children to know that He is not a foreign God. It was important to Him and that is why God told her to look at the scroll.

At that time, this family's concept of Christianity was turned upside-down! They realized for the first time that, as Christians, they were not accepting a foreign God but were coming home to their True God! They had thought that the Christian God they accepted never cared for their people and dwelt elsewhere; now they realized that He had placed them in Japan and was always near to them, loving them and hoping that they would reach out to Him (Acts 17:26-28). It was their ancestors, as the priests of Japan, who had led their people away from Him! (Romans 1:20-23) They realized that they needed to repent of the sins of their ancestors and return home to Him! (2 Chronicles 7:14) Their God had made a way for this to happen through the sacrifice of His Son, Jesus Christ.

Shades of Moke and Hawai'i! And the adventure continues!

---

All of the people who were involved with the 'Io Project that we contacted for this book still say that being involved with the 'Io Project was an indescribable experience in the intimate presence of God, one of the highest points in their lives, and a life-changing experience they will never forget.

# 26
# Postscript

On March 14, 1998, in obedience to God, nearly a hundred teams of Hawaiian Followers of Jesus on all of the major Hawaiian Islands went to the human sacrifice heiau(s) and repented to 'Io for the shedding of innocent human blood. More miracles happened in nature and in the Spirit than any of us had ever seen.

Because there were so many specific things that God told people to do at each site (each was different), the majority were omitted from this book. Many people who had important roles in this project are not even mentioned. Nearly 100 teams went out across the islands to over 125 sites on March

14. Intercessors in Hawai'i and around the world also had words, visions and dreams from God about the event. Many things that happened during the two years of research, planning and prayer before the project also are not recorded.

We saw many things that we did not know how to place in our Western Christian theology. However, too many people saw them, had visions of them or heard the Lord speak of them for us to ignore them.

Many heard people weeping and smelled fresh blood. It seemed like the land was crying out to be cleansed and miracles in the sky, land and sea occurred when it was cleansed. Whirlwinds, lights, birds singing, crashing waves calming, and many other phenomena not recorded in this book occurred.

People may ask why we do not have more pictures of these phenomena. One must remember that we were not going out as spiritual tourists; we were going out as warriors on assignment, fighting against a supernaturally powerful foe. We needed to focus fully on what we were doing and listen closely to God's directions with no distractions. I had warned people that the distraction of taking movies or photos could jeopardize the mission and the teams' safety. Besides, photos can always be doctored. People who choose not to believe this story would not be convinced by having more photos.

To those who have a personal relationship with Jesus Christ and obey Him, the events in this book are not hard to believe at all. They are normal occurrences for them. These events are really easy things for an omnipotent God! Although the 'Io Project was the largest project we've been a part of, we have had many similar adventures with God before the 'Io Project and since then. How exciting and fulfilling life with Christ is!

I haved teased my friend Moke, saying he is the only one I know who was called into his ministry 800 years ago. Now that specific ministry role is done.

Moke did not want his real name or the real name and location of 'Iokāne heiau revealed for these reasons:

1. He didn't want people looking to him. His priestly duties at 'Iokāne are over. He has turned 'Iokāne over to the great high priest, Iesū Kristo. He didn't want people to look to a flawed man and a priesthood that was just a shadow of what was fulfilled in Iesū Kristo. Why follow man when you can have a personal relationship with God? If you look to man, you will be disappointed or led astray. And as I have mentioned in the introduction, being famous is not a Hawaiian value, but being pono is.

2. Moke didn't want spiritual tourists swarming 'Iokāne trying to "deify" that place and make it an icon. When Jesus died on the cross for our sins, the veil in the temple which separated the people from the presence of God ripped from top to bottom. In the same way, God ripped open the dark clouds, the veil of sin and bondage over Hawai'i so people in Hawai'i can now freely commune with Him. Jesus said in John 4:21 and 23 (KJV) "... *believe me, the hour cometh, when ye shall neither in this mountain, nor yet at Jerusalem, worship the Father. But the hour cometh, and now is, when the true worshippers shall worship the Father in spirit and in truth: for the Father seeketh such to worship him.*"

If we accept Jesus, the Holy Spirit of God will come and dwell in us. We can then have a personal relationship with God all the time and anywhere. There is no need to seek after and lift up Moke or 'Iokāne as some "idol." We need to worship God in Spirit and in Truth all the time and anywhere. We are now the "'Iokāne of God!" I Corinthians 6:19 (NKJV) says, "*Or do you not know that your body is the temple of the Holy Spirit who is in you, whom you have from God, and you are not your own? For you were bought at a price; therefore glorify God in your body and in your spirit, which are God's.*"

I want to also mention here that I am not a person to follow either. I have done nothing that is not available to anyone who has a personal relationship with Jesus; and a personal relationship with Jesus is available to anyone, anytime.

My identity needed to be known so I could fulfill my new assignment from God: to tell all people that He has this same story of love and faithfulness for them, too.

---

Missionary Richie Lambeth finished his report by saying, "*I had just witnessed a miracle of extreme magnitude [his experience at 'Iokāne]. There was a seed of Holy Zeal that was planted in the earth in Kohala that day by the Holy Spirit and it has been germinating in its bowels ever since. Soon it will sprout and grow into one of the most incredible revivals that the earth has ever experienced. True Aloha is coming to cover the Islands of Hawai'i! Jesus Christ is coming to establish His Throne and His Righteousness will truly perpetuate the life of this land!*"

Now that this tap root sin in Hawai'i has been dealt with, God could plant new seeds into deep fertile soil instead of soil that was cursed to barrenness. What kinds of fruits, herbs and flowers did 'Io plant in his new garden? What dormant seeds from the past can now germinate because of the good soil and the new rain of the Holy Spirit? What will sprout from the golden spheres of His anointing that were spread across Hawai'i on March 14, 1998?

We have reclaimed stewardship of the land; now we are responsible for it before God. As we, the hands of God on earth, tend to His garden and continue clearing out the more recent weeds and "sin pollution," we wait patiently to see what kinds of fruits appear and what flowers bloom in God's time. We watch expectantly as God's plan for the islands slowly unfolds before us. Many wonderful and amazing things are beginning to "sprout up" throughout the islands; there are changes in people's hearts, changes in the 'āina (land), the Hawaiian community, the church, the government, agriculture, business and our schools that we would have never imagined possible. Many of the sites that were prayed over are being restored to fruitfulness. I do not want to "trumpet" about the particular people and places that are in the process of restoration here. These "sprouts" are still young and fragile and can wither away. They need to be protected from marauding spiritual predators desiring to suck their new life for their own gain or gnaw at them until they fall. If they survive, God will make their fruit known in His time, like He did with the events in this book.

The story of Hawai'i continues! There are tremendous challenges and much work still lies ahead of us. Many sins of the church and the people of Hawai'i still need to be dealt with and made pono. We have only just begun!

Aloha Ke Akua! (God is Love!),
*Daniel Kikawa*

# Endnotes

## Chapter One

1. 'Io or 'Ia was the name the Polynesians called the Creator God. The following portions of a Maori sacred chant of creation are compared to Genesis 1 in the King James Version (KJV).

    "'Io dwelt within the breathing space of immensity. The universe was in darkness, with water everywhere. There was no glimmer of dawn, no clearness, no light. And He began by saying these words, that He might cease remaining inactive, 'Darkness, become a light-possessing darkness.' And at once light appeared" (Handy, *Ancient Hawaiian Civilization*, pp. 43-45).

    Genesis 1:2-3 says, "And the earth was without form, and void; and darkness was upon the face of the deep. And the Spirit of God moved upon the face of the waters. And God said, 'Let there be light: and there was light.' "

    "...'Io then looked to the waters which compassed Him about and spake a fourth time, saying, 'Ye waters of Tai-kama, be ye separate. Heaven be formed.' Then the sky became suspended. 'Bring forth thou Tupu-horo-nuku.' And at once the moving earth lay stretched abroad" (Handy, *Ancient Hawaiian Civilization*, pp. 43-45).

    Genesis 1:6-9 says, "And God said, 'Let there be a firmament in the midst of the waters, and let it divide the waters from the waters. And God made the firmament, and divided the waters which were under the firmament from the waters which were above the firmament: and it was so. And God called the firmament Heaven. And the evening and the morning were the second day. And God said, Let the waters under the heaven be gathered together unto one place, and let the dry land appear: and it was so."

    The notable Polynesian historian, Sir Peter Buck, counted 27 different names for 'Io. (Handy, *Ancient Hawaiian Civilization*, p. 444). A few of these names and their meanings are compared with biblical descriptions of God:

    'Io-matua: He is the parent of all things, natural phenomena, plants, animals, man, and gods.

Colossians 1:16 says, "*For by Him were all things created, that are in heaven, and that are in earth, visible and invisible...*"

'Io-matua-kore: He had no parents, "*He was nothing but Himself.*"

(Hebrew) Yahweh: meaning. The Self- Existent One. Exodus 3:14: "*...I AM THAT I AM...*"

'Io-te-wananga: He is the source of all knowledge.

Colossians 2:3: "*In whom are hid all the treasures of wisdom and knowledge.*"

'Io-mata-ngaro: His face is hidden and unseen.

Exodus 33:20, "*And he said, Thou canst not see my face: for there shall no man see me, and live.*"

'Io-te-waiora: He is the source and giver of life.

Psalm 36:9, "*For with thee is the fountain of life:*"

'Io-mata-wai: 'Io, the God of love.

John 3:16, "*For God so loved the world, that he gave his only begotten Son, that whosoever believeth in him should not perish, but have everlasting life.*"

Another name for 'Io was 'Ia. One of the titles of 'Ia was 'Iaonalaninuiamamao, 'Ia of the great and distant heavens.

"*Sing unto God, sing praises to His name: extol Him that rideth upon the heavens by His name JAH, and rejoice before Him*" (Psalm 68:4 kjv).

2. In the mid-1970s, the Polynesian Voyaging Society was formed (pvs. hawaii.org) and a voyaging canoe built in the ancient design to prove the accuracy of wayfinding. This navigational method charts direction by observing the stars, ocean swells and currents, winds and clouds, birds and sea creatures, and even the taste, feel and smell of the ocean. A good navigator was highly valued by his tribe. The Hawaiian voyaging canoe was called the Hōkūleʻa, after the star that marked their ancestors' way to Hawaiʻi. In 1976 Hōkūleʻa navigator Mau Piailug proved without a doubt the accuracy of wayfinding by sailing to Tahiti and returning without the aid of modern instruments. Since then, the Hōkūleʻa, and two other canoes built in the old design, the Hawaiʻiloa and the Makaliʻi, have sailed many times across the Pacific to the islands of their Polynesian cousins.

3. The Polynesians had already traveled thousands of miles before reaching Hawaiʻi.

Some Hawaiian family chants and traditions say their ancestors sailed all the way from the great rivers of the heartland of civilization, possibly the Tigris and Euphrates rivers. These chants describe landmarks and resting places along the way that could correspond to India and Southeast Asia. Polynesians also left their mark in a type of design called "Lapita" found on pottery shards from Southeast

Asia to the Marquesas Islands on the far east of Polynesia. Shards found in the Marquesas are made of clay that comes from only one place, the Rewa Delta in Fiji. (Siers, *Tonga*, p.5) This provides strong evidence that these people had sailed accurately and frequently across thousands of miles of open ocean at a time when Western mariners were afraid to leave coastal waters lest they fall off of the earth at the horizon. Hawai'i, the most remote spot on earth, is over 2,000 miles from the nearest land mass. It has also been described as "the ends of the earth," the farthest place on earth from the Middle Eastern cradle of civilization and the last place occupied by man, sometime around 400 AD.

4. A heiau is a Hawaiian temple of worship. These temples were built of stacked stones. Heiau(s)* could be of different shapes and sizes but most were roughly rectangular. There was never a roof or ceiling to these temples, they were more of an enclosure, although there were roofs over certain structures within them. Some of them were massive with terraced levels which caused some foreign observers to describe them as "pyramids." They were sometimes built to pray for good fishing, a good harvest, or a safe journey, among other things. In the beginning, they were only built to worship the benevolent Creator, 'Io. In later years, they were built to worship many gods and even used for human sacrifice.

** (s) signifies plural. In Hawaiian language, words are pluralized by being preceded by the article "na," as opposed to the singular which is preceded by the articles "ka" or "ke."

## Chapter Two

1. The island of Hawai'i is today called the Big Island. It is a relative term. Compared to other land masses, it is just a small dot of land amidst 2000 miles of ocean. But compared to other islands in the Hawaiian chain, it is massive. All the other islands can fit into its land mass nearly twice.

2. The Hawaiians believed there were two kinds of thinking or knowledge. That which came from the po'o or head (head knowledge) which was called no'ono'o, and that which came from the na'au or the "gut" (gut knowledge or intuition) which was called mana'o. The Hawaiians knew these came from different sources because, many times, they would contradict each other. If one learned to listen to his na'au correctly (many times emotions were mistaken for true mana'o), he would find it was usually correct or even always correct. Therefore, although each one had its place and function, if they were conflicting, one's mana'o was to be taken over one's no'ono'o.

3. *Pono:* the word has no equal in the English language; It is translated in the Hawaiian dictionary as goodness, uprightness, morality, correct, proper, excellence, righteous, virtuous and many other words such as these. All of them fall short of the true meaning of the word. Even Hawaiians today use the word in ways bordering on sacrilege. The spiritual depth of the word is lost in today's polite niceties like "*Malama pono,*" "Take care." The closest description of pono that can be articulated in English is "in perfect order."

4. *Pa'a* meant strong and steady; to double it in Hawaiian meant to emphasize that trait. Hawaiians had names for all of their winds. At the wayfinders training heiau on Kaho'olawe (a tiny islet off of Maui) there was a point of land where a trained navigator could discern 42 different types of winds, each one with its own name. (Wood, Hana Hou! Magazine, *The Way Forward,* p. 70, Kahu Hanalei Colleado) Of course, if one was not attuned to the 'aina one would not even notice. Areas of Hawai'i were known by their particular wind, rain or sea current. A Hawaiian could say, "*Ka ua kani lehua*" meaning, "*The rain that sounds upon the leaves of the lehua trees.*" This was a rain so heavy that the pattering upon the leaves of the lehua trees, so abundant in Hilo, can almost become a roar. All would know he was talking about Hilo where this particular rain fell. So it was known that if one spoke of the 'Apa'apa'a winds, he was speaking of North Kohala.

5. The worship of 'Io was already corrupted in most of Hawai'i when Pā'ao arrived. The oral histories tell us that the famous navigator and chief, Hema, left Hawai'i to keep his worship of 'Io pure (Taylor, *Paradise of the Pacific,* Dec. 1931, p. 78). The Hawaiian historian, Kamakau, says Hema went to Aotearoa, New Zealand (Beckwith, Haw'n Myth., p. 241). Even so, it seems the Hawaiians lived in relative peace until Pā'ao came. Fornander writes of this period that "...the *kapus* were few and the ceremonials easy; that human sacrifices were not practised, and cannibalism unknown; and that government was more of a patriarchal than of a regal nature" (Fornander, *Acct. Poly. Race,* vol. 1, p. 209).

6. Handy, *Ancient Hawaiian Civilization,* pp. 43-45.

7. Fornander, *Acct. Poly. Race, vol. 1,* p. 62.

8. Pukui, *Hawaiian Dictionary.*
   Milner, *Samoan Dictionary.*

9. Kepelino/Beckwith, *Kepelino's Traditions of Hawai'i,* p.34.
   Fornander, *Acct. Poly. Race, vol. 1,* pp. 91, 225-235.
   Beckwith, *Hawaiian Mythology,* pp. 314-316.

## Chapter Three

1. Most historians estimate that Pā'ao came to Hawai'i around A.D. 1200. Oral histories say he came from Upolu and also possessed lands at Vavau. This led early historians to conclude he was from Upolu, one of the major islands of Samoa and Vavau, one of the major islands of Tonga about 350 miles to the south. We now know, through the excellent book by Rudy Mitchell, "From God to God," that it was far more likely that he came from the Society Islands (Tahiti) for several good reasons: the island Taha'a in western Tahiti was once called Upolu, (Mitchell, From God to God, Book II, Porapora, p. 5); the ancient name of Bora Bora, a close neighbor which can be seen from *Taha'a, was Vavau* (Mitchell, From God to God, Book II, Pā'ao, pp. 4-7). Rudy Mitchell and Hawaiian kupuna Aunty Malia Craver, both distant descendants of Pā'ao, visited Bora Bora and found their relatives by comparing genealogies (Mitchell, From God to God, Book II, Pā'ao, pp. 7-11). Also, the religious rituals and royal vestments of western Tahiti and those of the Hawaiian royalty established by Pā'ao are remarkably similar while the Samoan and Tonga rituals are not (Mitchell, From God to God, Book II, Pā'ao, pp. 12-14). Mitchell writes that Pā'ao was a kahuna nui (high priest), ali'i nui (high chief), famous navigator and a sorcerer of great power.

2. Both Malia Craver and Ahuena Taylor, whose families knew of 'Io, are descended from the lines of Pā'ao and Pili.

3. The points of the Polynesian Triangle were Hawai'i, Rapa Nui (Easter Island) and Aotearoa (New Zealand).

4. The Hawaiian historian, George Kaimiola, visited Tahiti in 2004 and inquired about the technique. He was told that gourds filled with air were tied to the ends of the paddles and were submerged under the water. The buoyancy would push the paddle upward and the paddler would push it back down, like a hydraulic piston. Thus, the blade of the paddle never broke the surface and no splashing or sound occurred.

5. Mitchell, *From God to God*, pp. 3-4.
   Malia Craver was told by her elders that Pā'ao brought many warriors and probably conquered the Hawaiian Islands in the same way his family did in Tahiti, with stealth and skilled warriors.

6. Before Pā'ao arrived, earlier voyagers from Tahiti integrated peacefully with the first inhabitants of Hawai'i. Apparently, there was intermarriage with these inhabitants and the diminishing of class distinction between the Tahitian ali'i and the commoners.

The oral histories say that when Pā'ao first visited Hawai'i; he regarded the Tahitian high chief of Hawai'i, Kapawa, a degenerate. The priests and ali'i(s) were not performing the rituals they had formerly performed in Tahiti to retain mana (divine power). They did not build the necessary heiau(s), perform the necessary human sacrifices, or wear the red feather malo (belt - the symbol of royalty in Ra'iatea) of high chiefs.

Pā'ao saw the islands as ripe for conquest. There were no powerful chiefly families or armies of trained warriors. He returned to Ra'iatea to bring a new line of ali'i with untainted "mana," spiritual authority and power. Pā'ao returned to Hawai'i not only with many warriors but with the ali'i, Pili. Through conquest and intermarriage with the older lines, Pili became powerful in the islands (Buck, Vikings of the Pacific, pp. 262-263).

To consolidate his power, Pā'ao instituted human sacrifices and changed the Hawaiians' religious rituals. He built the first luakini (human sacrifice) heiau on the Big Island at Waha'ula below the active crater at Kīlauea (Clark/Hon. Advertiser, *Number's Up for Heiau on Kīlauea's Hit List*).

7. By looking at the oral traditions and genealogies of the Polynesians, some historians believe Pā'ao lived for over 200 years. Some say he could have achieved this by eating the "mana" of other men, sucking out their life force into himself. Although the family of Pā'ao was originally from Bora Bora, they joined forces with the chiefly clan of Ra'iatea and eventually resided in the district of Opoa in Ra'iatea. This was where any priest of his clan must eventually go as it was the center of worship of the war god 'Oro. 'Oro, son of Ta'aroa, is said to have been born in Opoa.

8. Ta'aroa (D. Kawaharada, *1992 Voyage: Sail to Ra'iatea*, Polynesian Voyaging Society, http://pvs.kcc.Hawai'i.edu/1992/Ra'iatea.html), is said to have been born in Opoa. Ta'aroa (Tahitian), Tangaroa (Maori), Tangaloa (Tonga and Samoa), Tanaoa (Marquesan), Kanaloa (Hawaiian) were different Polynesian dialects for the same god. This god is not to be confused with Polynesian ancestors with the same name. Known as the creator god in central Polynesia, he was, to the remnant of the worshippers of 'Io, the great enemy of the true creator god. Kanaloa was called, in the Kumulipo, the evil smelling squid, Ka-he'e-hauna-wela. The ancient Polynesians believed a giant octopus or squid covered the far flung islands of Polynesia, its tentacles reaching out to the extremes of the Polynesian triangle. The head of the octopus and center of the triangle was at Taputapuatea. The evil smelling squid, Ta'aroa, controlled all of Polynesia from its center,

either himself or through his son, 'Oro, who seems to have manifested himself as an evil reincarnation of the god, Kū, in Hawai'i and, Tu, in Aotearoa (New Zealand.)

According to the Hawaiian historian, Kepelino, Kanaloa was the personified spirit of evil, the originator of death, and the Prince of Pō (Darkness or the Void). Kepelino described Pō as a place of *"unending fire and of strange impenetrable darkness."* It was a place where the spirits of the people who fall there were *"lost and they became hideous."* It was *"death without measure, night without measure, weeping without measure, and the dwelling place without end."* (Kepelino, *Kepelino's Trad. Of Hi.*, p. 48)

One major difference between Ta'aroa and 'Io was that man was sacred to 'Io and not to be killed but Ta'aroa demanded human sacrifice (Oliver, *Ancient Tahitian Society*, vol. 2, pp. 883, 909-911/D. Kawaharada, *1992 Voyage: Sail to Ra'iatea*, Polynesian Voyaging Society, http://pvs.kcc.Hawai'i.edu/1992/Ra'iatea.html). The nature of Ta'aroa is made clear in this ancient Tahitian official chant for the casting off of a "god."

*"There is a casting off, I am casting thee off. Do not come in to possess me again; let me not be a seat for thee again! Let me not know thee again; do thou not know me again. Go and seek some other medium for thyself in another home. Let it not be me, not at all! I am wearied of thee. I am terrified with thee! I am expelling thee. Go ever to the Vai-tu-pō (River-in-darkness), into the presence of Ta'aroa, thy father, Ta'aroa, the father of all gods. Return not again to me. Behold the family, they are stricken with sickness; thou art taking them, thou art a terrible man-devouring god!"* (Buck, *The Coming of the Maori*, p. 520.)

How different this is from 'Io-mata-wai, the God of Mercy! How different were Kāne, the part of the Hawaiian trinity through whom creation occurred, and 'Oro, the son of Ta'aroa? Kāne made man in his own image; man was sacred to him and not to be killed. 'Oro, the son of Ta'aroa, on the other hand, demanded the blood of men.

There is some evidence that Pā'ao's Marai (temple/heiau) at Taputapuatea was first dedicated to 'Io until the 'Io worshippers were overcome by the Ta'aroa/'Oro worshippers (from the thinly veiled Maori history in the novel, *Behind the Tattooed Face*, Heretaunga Baker, pp. 97-102). According to oral tradition, those who settled the other Tahitian Islands (Society islands), and those who migrated to other places like Hawai'i and New Zealand, fled Ra'iatea because of the tyrannical rule of the priests of 'Oro who demanded strict kapu (taboos) be kept on pain of death and numerous human sacrifices

(Oliver, *Ancient Tahitian Society*, Vol. 2, p. 779). Maori traditions of 'Io reveal that their ancestors fled "Rangiatea" when they were attacked by a more powerful tribe.

When Taputapuatea became dedicated to 'Oro human sacrifices increased in number and frequency (D. Kawaharada, *1992 Voyage: Sail to Ra'iatea*, Polynesian Voyaging Society, http://pvs.kcc.Hawai'i. edu/1992/Ra'iatea.html). It is said that more humans were sacrificed at Taputapuatea than at any other temple in Polynesia. When Taputapuatea was excavated, it was found that the spaces between the walls were filled with skulls from sacrifices.

9. Fornander wrote that *"...there was a time before that, when human sacrifices were not only not of common occurrence, ... but were absolutely prohibited. Kapu ke kanaka na Kāne, 'sacred is the man to Kāne...'"* (Fornander, *Acct. Poly. Race*, vol. 1, p. 209) Kāne was one of the ancient benign trinity of Polynesia, made up of Kū, Kāne and Lono, who were really aspects of the one supreme God, 'Io. Fornander wrote, *"...I learn that the ancient Hawaiians at one time believed in and worshipped one God, comprising three beings, and respectively called Kāne, Kū and Lono, equal in nature, but distinct in attributes."* (Fornander, *Acct. Poly. Race*, vol. 1, p. 218) All three were corrupted by Pā'ao's religious system, especially Kū.

Hawaiian legends say the triune God's last accomplishment on the sixth day of creation was to create man in the likeness of Kāne. Hence, man is also called Kāne. In the Marquesas, the first man is called Atea (meaning – The Light) after the creator of men, Atea, who corresponds to Kāne in Hawai'i. The body of the first man was made of red earth and when the clay image of Kāne was ready, the three gods breathed into his nose and he became a living being. (Fornander, *Acct. Poly. Race*, vol. 1, pp. 70-71/Beckwith, *Haw'n Myth.*, pp. 42-46) Genesis 2:7 (KJV) says, *"And the Lord God formed man of the dust of the ground, and breathed into his nostrils the breath of life; and man became a living soul."*

The Hawaiian traditions state that Kanaloa (Ta'aroa) led a rebellion against the triune God, because he and his minions were not allowed to drink 'awa ('awa implies worship). They were defeated by Kāne and cast down to the underworld where Kanaloa, became the ruler of the dead. Kāne drew the figure of a man in the earth and Kanaloa made one also. Kāne's man lived but Kanaloa's did not; making Kanaloa very angry. He then made all kinds of poisonous things and cursed man to die (Kepelino. *Kepelino's Trad. Of Hi.*, p. 48).

## Chapter Four

1. Fornander wrote, "*In the polity of government initiated during this period, and strengthened as ages rolled on, may be noted the hardening and confirming the divisions of society, the exaltation of the nobles and the increase of their prerogatives, the separation and immunity of the priestly order, and the systematic setting down, if not actual debasement, of the commoners, the Maka'āinana*" (Fornander, Acct. Poly. Race, vol. 2, p. 63). The class separation between the ali'i(s) with their "divine" mana and the common Hawaiian became a huge gulf.

   What most people today regard as the religious system of the old Hawaiian people, was not their true religion—it was a foreign religion introduced by the invader Pā'ao.

   Pā'ao's voyages from Tahiti were the last from other Polynesian islands. The Tahitian historian, Teuira Henry, wrote that an alliance of Polynesian islands ended around 600 years ago because of a dispute at a meeting of navigators. The navigators from the different Polynesian islands never met again. By the time Captain Cook arrived in Hawai'i, canoe voyages to other Polynesian Islands were merely a tradition (Krauss, Hon. Advertiser, Sun. Jan. 15, 1995, p. D2).

2. When Pā'ao arrived in Hawai'i, he brought the Ta'aroa Cult from Tahiti; placing Ta'aroa (Kanaloa in Hawaiian) as a major god along side of the Hawaiian trinity of Kū, Kāne and Lono. Although the original trinity of Hawaiian gods was already degraded when Pā'ao arrived, they became but corrupted shadows of their former selves under Pā'ao, especially the God, Kū. At some unknown time after Pā'ao arrived, the benign god, Kū, was changed into a reincarnation of 'Oro, the vengeful and bloodthirsty god of war (Pukui, Nānā, p. 122/Fornander, Acct. Poly. Race, vol. 1, p. 163). Although more refined in features than 'Oro, the personal Kū, god of Kamehameha, Kūkā'ilimoku, was an inverted sennit basket woven in the shape of a man and covered with feathers; as some 'Oro images were. This type of 'Oro image was called, 'Oro-hu'a-manu, "Oro of the bird-feathered body" (Oliver, *Ancient Tahitian Society*, vol. 2, p. 904).

   According to the Hawaiian historian Samuel Kamakau, Kūkā'ilimoku was brought from Tahiti to Hawai'i by Pā'ao (Valerio, trans. Wissing, *Kingship and Sacrifice*, p. 247). However, according to Fornander, the name of Kūkā'ilimoku does not appear until many generations later (Valerio, trans. Wissing, *Kingship and Sacrifice*, p. 247). It is very possible that the god Kamakau mentions was 'Oro who later "morphed" into Kūkā'ilimoku. Although Kū in his different forms was well known as the God of War, it is not as well known that he was also the god of sorcery. Beckwith states that *"All the images of war gods named under the Kū group are in fact sorcery gods."* (Valerio, trans. Wissing, *Kingship and Sacrifice*, p. 247) Like the Kālaipāhoa sorcery gods and all gods used by sorcerers, Kūkāʻilimoku and the related Ku gods sometimes appeared as akualele, the flying fireballs, when they were sent to devour someone (Valerio, trans. Wissing, *Kingship and Sacrifice*, p. 247).

3. The Mū(s) were the official executioners of the kahuna. They procured the human sacrifices who were usually a captured enemy or a kapu breaker. If an enemy was not captured or someone did not break a kapu, the Mū(s) were sent out to find a sacrifice. Parents would threaten their children to behave or the Mū would get them! (Pukui/ Elbert, *Hawaiian Dictionary*, p. 255)

4. The common people owned no land under the Kapu System—in fact, they had no rights and *nothing* they could call their own. An aliʻi could take anything he wanted from a commoner: his food, his belongings, his favorite pig, his children—or even his wife. The aliʻi could "tax" most of a commoner's food away and force him to work on his building projects. It is estimated that two-thirds of what the common people produced was taken by high aliʻi(s) and kahuna(s). The common people were so maltreated and malnourished that, when the first anthropologists arrived, they thought that the Hawaiians were composed of two different races - the huge aliʻi and the scrawny common people! (Montgomery, *Christus Redemptus*, pp. 95,97/Malo, *Antiquities*, pp. 62,64/ Kamakau, *Ruling Chiefs of Hi.*, pp. 229-232)

   Not only were these harsh requirements put on the common people but they were repeatedly forced into armies to fight whenever their aliʻi(s) wanted more power. Captured commoners were used as slaves or for sacrifices. The Hawaiian population was decimated by these wars. By the time of Kamehameha, there had been some 300 years of nearly constant warfare. (Emerson, *Pioneer Days in Hi.*, p. 4)

   In 1826, reporting what he had observed during his forty-nine years in Hawaiʻi, John Young, Kamehameha's trusted foreign advisor said, *"I have known thousands of defenseless human beings cruelly massacred in their exterminating wars. I have seen multitudes…offered in sacrifice to their idol gods…"* (Piercy, *Hawaiʻi Truth Stranger Than Fiction*, p. 40)

5. Using this new religious system created by Pāʻao, the aliʻi(s) convinced the common people that their families had inherited divine power (mana) and, therefore, they were divinely chosen by the gods to rule. The Kapu System was built upon the theory of protecting mana (spiritual power). Complicated kapu(s), laws, had to be instituted

to preserve the mana and maintain its balance in the 'āina for it to be fruitful. These laws controlled every aspect of life to maintain the balance and stability of the mana. If a kapu was broken, the way the mana was stabilized usually required the death of the kapu breaker. While some kapu(s) encouraged the wise use of resources, the social/ political aspects of the kapu system provided an open door for abuse. High ali'i were never put to death for breaking a kapu, however, commoners were sometimes sacrificed to correct the "imbalance in the mana" caused by the "sin" of an ali'i. The common people had no control or input about who came to power. It was very rare indeed for the common people to overthrow an ali'i, and only another ali'i could take his place. Although there were exceptions, the majority of the ali'i(s) and kahuna(s) used their power for personal gain and not for the good of the people (Montgomery, *Christus Redemptus*, pp.94, 97/ Malo, *Antiquities*, pp. 56-58, 60-61).

An ali'i could take commoners who committed "sins" and use them for shark hunting (Kamakau, *Ruling Chiefs of Hi.*, pp. 232,236). There were ovens for burning humans at Punchbowl Crater (where the War Memorial of the Pacific stands today) and at Waikiki (Kamakau, *Ruling Chiefs of Hi.*, p. 232,236/ Sterling/Summers, *Sites of O'ahu*, p. 291). Commoners were drowned at Kewalo Basin (Honolulu) for breaking a kapu. (Sterling/Summers, *Sites of O'ahu*, p. 292) The heads of sacrifice victims were impaled on stakes that lined the Pakaka heiau at the foot of Fort Street (Downtown Honolulu). (McAllister, *Archaeology of O'ahu*, p. 81) At the heiau located at the Waikiki end of Diamond Head, men had their arms and legs broken with clubs, their eyes scooped out, and then were left bleeding and maimed for three days. They were later sacrificed, clubbed to death by blows to the shoulders rather than to the head, thus prolonging their suffering before death (McAllister, *Archaeology of O'ahu*, p. 71).

6. Potter/Kasdon, *Hawai'i Our Island State*, p. 46.

7. Valeri, trans. Wissing, *Kingship and Sacrifice*, p. 181

8. Handy believed that the "Kanaloa cult" was introduced by a later migration of people. He says: "The hypothesis that Tangaloa was introduced later than Tu, Tane, and Rongo is alone capable of explaining his position in different sections of Polynesia. In the three main groups of islands on the outer margin of this area (Hawai'i, the Marquesas, New Zealand) he appears in the genealogies as a descendant from the marriage of Heaven and Earth. He was also a deity of prime importance in both mythology and worship, *but was never elevated to the position of creator*. On the other hand, in the three main

groups in the central and western region of Polynesia (Samoa, Tonga, and the Society Islands) he was regarded as the preexistent Supreme Being who originated all things."(author's emphasis) (Handy, Polynesian Religion, B. 34, p. 324).

9. Valeri, trans. Wissing, *Kingship and Sacrifice*, pp.247-248, 402.

10. Fornander says that Pele worship in Hawai'i is only subsequent to this migratory period. *"The Pele cult was unknown to the purer faith of the older inhabitants and her name does not even appear in creation accounts of the Hawaiians."* (Kikawa, *Perpetuated In Righteousness*, p. 142).

11. Valeri, trans. Wissing, *Kingship and Sacrifice*, pp. 336-339.

12. Valeri, trans. Wissing, *Kingship and Sacrifice*, p. 87.

13. Valeri, trans. Wissing, *Kingship and Sacrifice*, pp. 57-58, 322.

## Chapter Five

1. John Kūpuna (an alias), who was told by his father about the secret ways of his kahuna 'anā'anā ancestors.

2. passed down to Akea Eaton from his kūpuna who had witnessed this.

3. passed down to Akea Eaton from his kūpuna who had witnessed these things.

## Chapter Six

1. Gessler, *Hawai'i, Isles of Enchantment*, p. 58.

2. Honolulu Star Bulletin, *All About Hawai'i*, pp. 28-29.

3. Mitchell, *From God to God*, p. 33 / the Hawaiian Music Foundation Web site. http://www.hawaiimusicmuseum.org/honorees/2000/chanters.html

4. Gough, ed., *To the Pacific and Arctic with Beechey: The Journal of Lieutenant George Peard of H.M.S. Blossom, 1825-1828*, p. 135.

5. Brewster, *Memoir of Ke'opuolani*, p. 17.

6. Piercy, *Hawai'i's Missionary Saga*, p. 19, Hewahewa's thoughts mirror what Paul told the Athenians in Acts 17:28-29 (EB), *"We live in him. We walk in him. We are in him.' Some of your own poets have said: 'For we are his children.' We are God's children. So you must not think that God is like something that people imagine or make. He is not like gold, silver, or rock."*

7. Taylor, *Kapi'olani: A Memorial*, pp. 15-16.

8. Dwight, *Memoirs of Henry Obookiah.*

9. Gessler, *Hawai'i, Isles of Enchantment*, p. 58
   Kailua-Kona Walking Tour Brochure.

10. Mitchell, *From God to God*, p. 36.

## Chapter Seven

1. Piercy, *Hawai'i Truth*, p. 115.

2. Passed down to Aunty Malia Craver by her Kūpuna.

3. Marocco, *Hawai'i's Great Awakening*, p. 17.

4. Twain, M. *Roughing It.*

## Chapter Eight

1. Loomis, *To All People*, pp. 24-25.

2. Dougherty, *To Steal a Kingdom*, p. 109
   Piercy, *Hawai'i Truth*, p. 14.

3. Oral history from Kahu John A. Kalili.

4. Lili'uokalani, like the Kāula before her, put her trust in God. While
   imprisoned by the usurpers, she wrote what has become known as the
   Queen's Prayer:
   "*Your love is in heaven,*
   *and your truth so perfect.*
   *I live in sorrow imprisoned,*
   *you are my light,*
   *your glory my support.*
   *Behold not with malevolence the sins of man*
   *but forgive and cleanse.*
   *And so, O Lord, beneath your wings*
   *be our peace forever more.*"

5. Lili'uokalani, *Hawai'i's Story*, p. xii.

6. Rennie Mau, former President of the Association of Hawai'i
   Evangelical Churches.

7. the website of the Hawaiian Music Foundation
   http://www.hawaiimusicmuseum.org/honorees/2000/chanters.html.

## Chapter Nine

1. The Bible states, "*What may be known about God is plain to men*
   *because God has made it plain to them. For since the creation of the world*

*God's invisible qualities—His eternal power and divine nature—have been clearly seen, being understood from what has been made, so that men are without excuse"* (Romans 1:20 NIV). This means that, from the creation of the world, if one wanted to find God, He was clearly seen in the creation around us. God's eternal power and His divine nature are so clear that men are without excuse if, after they pass from this world into the next, they stand before their Creator and say, *"But God, I was in the jungle alone and no one ever told me about you."*

What person would not want to know God's eternal power? What scholar would not want to understand his Godhead? It is something scholars with many letters after their names still argue about; obviously, they have not found all the answers in their books.

More modern Western Christians need to "waste" time like this, listening and learning from creation instead of watching television or movies, playing video games, and running to death on their rat race wheels!

*"From one man he (God) made every nation of men, that they should inhabit the whole earth; and he (God) determined the times set for them and the exact places where they should live. God did this so that men would seek him and perhaps reach out for him and find him, though he is not far from each one of us. For in him we live and move and have our being.... We are his offspring"* (Acts 17: 26-28 NIV). God placed all people where they should be and set the time of their habitation there. He placed them in the best environment for His particular children to find Him, whether in the jungles of Africa or on a dot of land surrounded by 2,000 miles of open ocean. He was near to His children, speaking to them, wooing them home, never far, surrounding them with His presence with every step and every breath.

2. This is similar to the lion, lamb, eagle, sun, etc. being symbols of Jesus and God in the Bible.

## Chapter Twelve

1. Mitchell, *From God to God, Porapora*, p. 4-5.

## Chapter Twenty-one

1. **Waiʻaleʻale I Na Mauna Lā**
   Waiʻaleʻale I Na Mauna Lā
   Waiʻaleʻale in the mountains

   Eia noho wāwae e lā
   The footstool (of the Creator)

E Hoʻomaʻemaʻe, I ka wā
To be cleansed at this time

E hoʻi mai, I ka ua lā
Returning of the rains

I ka waena o Kauaʻi lā
In the center of Kauaʻi

E hoʻomana o ʻIo lā ʻIo
(Sovereign One of the Universe) is worshipped

E mele no me ka haʻa lā
Songs of praise with humbleness

I hana kamahaʻo ana lā
At the wonderful hand (works) of the Holy One

Haʻina mai i na pua lā
This song is told to the children

He inoa poni wale lā
In the name of the Anointed One

Ea lā, ea lā, ea

He inoa no Ke Aliʻi o na aliʻi
In the Name of the King of Kings

## Chapter Twenty-two

1. K. Grant, *Hawaii.* Pp. 239-240

## Chapter Twenty-three

1. *Lord of the Islands*
   You're Lord of the Islands
   Ka Haku o na moku
   You're Lord of the valleys below
   Ka Haku o na awaawa
   You're Lord of the mountain top
   Ka Haku o na mauna
   Jesus be Lord of my life!
   Iesū ka Haku o ke ola
   And we reclaim the victory in Jesus!
   For we are washed by the blood of the Lamb!
   For here we stand in the presence of your Glory!

We've been redeemed by the blood of the Lamb!
© Wayne Santos (Hawaiian translation—Kaho'okele Crabbe) from
the CD "A Call to the Nations," Na Kahu—Aloha Ke Akua II

2. Oral history told to Akea Eaton.

3. "Pu'u 'Ōhelo" by Zennie Sawyer (The story of her experience on the
mountains above Hālawa Valley)
'Auhea 'oe
*Where are you?*
E ka niolo i ka wēkiu?
*O peak that rises to the heights?*
I nalo 'ia a heno 'ia 'oe e ka uhiwai
*Hidden and caressed by the mist spreading over you.*
Pohā ka lā a e 'ike lihi iā 'oe. E komo mai nei iā mākou.
*Sunlight breaks through beckoning, giving glimpses of you.*
'Auhea 'oe
*Where are you?*
E ka niolo i ka wēkiu
*O peak that rises to the heights?*
I ia wahi e maha ai ka haili moe.
*That spot where the vision lies.*
Pā maila ka makani a hi'ilawe,
*The wind swirls, carries us*
A hi'ipoi ia makou i ka poli o ka Haku
And sets us in the welcome of His bosom.
Ua kīpuni 'ia mākou e ka ohu kau kuahiwi
*Mist gently descends around and upon us*
Kulu ihola ke kēhau mai ka 'ohi'a mai
*Dew drips from 'ōhia trees*
Pulupē i ka honua la'a a mākou i hehi ai
*Drenching the ground as a cushion we dare to walk upon*
Pulupē nei i ka 'ili i ka 'olu o Kona hanu
*So sacred—we are moistened by the cool, wet breath of the Maker*
Lohe 'ia ke kī'ilili o nā manu i ka mālie
*Songs of the birds and the Kahuli woven in the stillness*
E ka niolo i ka wēkiu
*Of you, o peak that rises to the heights*
Ua ho'ola'i iā loko
*We are hushed within*
Ke hea mai e pūliki mai
*As we are called to embrace you*
I ka ma'e o Pu'u 'Ōhelo.
*In the purity at Pu'u 'Ōhelo.*

Pā mālie mai ke ala, he lei i hoʻowehi iā mākou
*So pleasant the fragrance that adorns us as a lei*
O ka pua lehua o ia wahi no ia
*Of the lehua blossoms in that place*
Pili hoʻi i Kona poli,
*How close to the One we seek,*
Me he ala he ʻanoʻi
*Gathered as lovers in His arms*
E maliu mai. E pohai ʻia ʻoe e Kona nani - ʻo ka hana no o Kona mau lima.
*A moment to share in the beauty of His hands*

   Kahe ihola! Kahe ihola!
   *Run down! Run down!*
   I ka papakū
   *To the depths within*
   E ala aʻe! E ala aʻe e ka wai ola
   *Rise up! Rise up! Life-giving water!*
   Mai kahi kūhohonu e hoʻomomona ʻia e ka Haku
   *From the bowels, that which the Maker has seeded*
   I ka niolo I ka wēkiu
   *To the peak that rises to the heights!*

ʻAuhea ʻoe
*Where are you*
E ka niolo i ka wēkiu?
*O peak that rises to the heights?*
Lohe ʻia Kona leo hawanawana, "ʻEia hoʻi au
*His whisper comes—"I am here;*
A eia ʻoe pū me aʻu.
*And you are here with Me."*
(Hawaiian translantion—Vanda Hanakahi)

# Bibliography

Allen, H. *The Betrayal of Lili'uokalani*. Glendale, CA: Mutual, 1982

Alpers, A. *The World of the Polynesians*. 1970; rpt. Auckland, N.Z.: Oxford University Press, 1987

Baker, H. *Behind the Tattooed Face*. New Zealand: Cape Catley Ltd., 1975

Beckwith, M. *Hawaiian Mythology*. 1940; rpt. Honolulu: University of Hawai'i Press, 1970

—. ed. *Kumulipo*. 1951; rpt. Honolulu: University Press of Hawai'i

Best, E. *The Maori As He Was*. Wellington, N.Z.: A.R. Shearer, Government Printer, 1974

—. *Maori Religion and Mythology*. No. 10-11. *Dominion Museum Bulletin*. Wellington, N.Z.: W.A.G. Skinner, Government Printer,1924

—. *The Astronomical Knowledge of the Maori*. No. 3. Dominion Museum Bulletin. Wellington, N. Z.: W.A.G. Skinner, Government Printer, 1922

Bingham, H. *A Residence of Twenty-One Years in the Sandwich Islands* Hartford: Hezekiah Huntington, 1847

Brandewie, E. *Wilhelm Schmidt and the Origin of the Idea of God*. Lanham, M.D.: University Press of America, 1983

Buck, P. *The Coming of the Maori*. Christchurch, N.Z.: Whitcombe & Tombs Ltd., 1949

—. *Vikings of the Pacific*. Chicago: University of Chicago Press, 1959

Coan, T. *Life In Hawai'i*. N.Y.: Anson D.F. Randolph & Co.,1882

Clark. "Number's Up for Heiau on Kilauea's Hit List." *Honolulu Advertiser*. Newspaper. Honolulu

Curtis C. *Builders of Hawai'i*. Honolulu: Kamehameha Schools, 1966

Davis, C. *The Life And Times Of Patuone*. Auckland, N.Z.: Steam Printing Co., 1876

Daws, G. *Shoal of Time*. Honolulu: University of Hawai'i Press, 1968

De Bovis, E., Craig R. trans. *Tahitian Society Before the Arrival of the Europeans*. Hawaii: Brigham Young University Press, 1976

Dougherty, M. *To Steal A Kingdom*. Waimanalo, Hi. : Island Style Press, 1992

Dwight, E. *Memoirs of Henry Obookiah*. Ed. Wolfe, E. Honolulu: Woman's Board of Missions for the Pacific Islands, 1990

Emerson, O.P. *Pioneer Days in Hawai'i*. New York: Doubleday, Doran & Co., 1928

Feher, J. *Hawai'i: A Pictorial History*. Honolulu: Bishop Museum, 1969

Fornander, A. *An Account of the Polynesian Race*. 3 vols. London, 1878-1885; rpt. Rutland, Vt. : Charles E. Tuttle Co., 1969

—. *Fornander Collection of Hawaiian Antiquities and Folk-lore*. vol. IV of the *Memoirs of the Bernice Pauahi Bishop Museum*. ed. Thrum, T. Honolulu: Bishop Museum, 1916-1917

—. *Fornander Collection of Hawaiian Antiquities and Folk-lore*. vol. V of the *Memoirs of the Bernice Pauahi Bishop Museum*. ed. Thrum,T. Honolulu: Bishop Museum, 1918-1919

—. *Fornander Collection of Hawaiian Antiquities and Folk-lore*. vol. VI of the *Memoirs of the Bernice Pauahi Bishop Museum*. Honolulu: Bishop Museum, 1919-1920

Gessler, C. *Hawai'i, Isles of Enchantment*. N.Y.: D. Appleton-Century, 1937

Gough, B. ed., *To the Pacific and Arctic with Beechey: The Journal of Lieutenant George Peard of H.M.S. Blossom, 1825-1828*. London: The Hakluyt Society, 1973

Grant, K., Bendure, G., Friary, N., Gorry, C. *Hawaii*. Oakland, CA: Lonely Planet, 2005

Handy, E.S.C. *Polynesian Religion*. Bul. 34. *Bishop Museum*. Honolulu: Bishop Museum,1927

—. "Religion and Education." in *Ancient Hawaiian Civilization, A Series of Lectures*. Ed. Pratt, H. Honolulu: Kamehameha Schools, 1933

—. *The Hawaiian Cult of 'Io*. vol. 50-51 *Journal of the Polynesian Society*. Wellington: The Polynesian Society, 1941

Handy, E.S.C. and Pukui, M.K. *The Polynesian Family System in Ka'ū, Hawai'i*. Wellington, N.Z.: Polynesian Society, 1958

Honolulu Star Bulletin. *All About Hawai'i*. Honolulu: Honolulu Star Bulletin, Feb. 1936

'Ī'Ī, J. *Fragments of Hawaiian History*. Trans. Pukui, M. Honolulu: Bishop

Museum Press, 1959

International Bible Society. *The Holy Bible, New International Version* Grand Rapids, MI: Zondervan, 1984

Irwin, G. *The Prehistoric Exploration and Colonisation of the Pacific* Cambridge, U.K.: Cambridge University Press, 1992

Kamakau, S. *Ruling Chiefs of Hawai'i*. Trans. Pukui, M., et al. Honolulu: Kamehameha School Press, 1961

Kamakau, S. *Tales and Traditions of the People of Old*. Trans. Pukui, M. Ed. Barre're, D. Honolulu: Bishop Museum Press, 1991

Kanahele, G. *Kū Kanaka*. Honolulu: University of Hawai'i Press, 1986

Kane, H. *The Voyagers*. Bellevue, WA.: WhaleSong, 1991

Kawaharada, D. 1992 Voyage: Sail to Ra'iatea, Polynesian Voyaging Society, http://pvs.kcc.hawaii.edu/1992/raiatea.html

Kepelino. *Kepelino's Traditions of Hawai'i*. Bulletin 95. *Bernice P. Bishop Museum*. Ed. Beckwith, M. 1932; rpt. Millwood, N.Y.: Kraus Reprint Co., 1978

—. Kepelino's "Hawaiian Collection": His "Hooiliili Havaii," Pepa I. vol. 11. The Hawaiian Journal of History. Trans. Kirtley, B. & Mookini, E. Ed. Jackson, F. 1858; rpt. Honolulu: Hawaiian Historical Society, 1977

Kikawa, D. *Perpetuated In Righteousness*, 4th Ed. Hawai'i: Aloha Ke Akua, 1994

Krauss, R. Honolulu Advertiser, Sun. Jan. 15, 1995

Kuykendall, R.S. *The Hawaiian Kingdom*. vol. II. Honolulu: University of Hawai'i Press, 1953

Kuykendall, R.S. *The Hawaiian Kingdom*. vol. III. Honolulu: University of Hawai'i Press, 1967

Lili'uokalani, L. *Hawai'i's Story by Hawai'i's Queen*. Honolulu: Mutual Publishing, 1990

Loomis, A. *By Faith*. Honolulu: Offset Printing House, 1980

Loomis, A. *To All People*. Tennessee: Hawai'i Conference of the United Church of Christ, 1970

Malo, D. *Hawaiian Antiquities*. Trans. Emerson, N. Honolulu: Bishop Museum Press, 1951

Marocco, J. *Hawaii's Great Awakening*. Bartimaeus Publishing. Kahului, Hi. , 1991

McAllister, J.G. *Archaeology of O'ahu*. Bulletin 104. *Bernice P. Bishop Museum*. 1933; rpt. Millwood, N.Y.: Kraus Reprint Co., 1971

Milner, G.B. *Samoan Dictionary*. 1966. rpt. Samoa: Gov't. of American Samoa, 1979

Mitchell, D. *Resource Units in Hawaiian Culture*. Honolulu: The Kamehameha Schools Press, 1982

Mitchell, R. *From God to God*. 3 Books. O'ahu: 1979

Montgomery, H. *Christus Redemptor*. MacMillan, 1906

Mulholland. *Hawai'i's Religions*. Rutland, Vt. : C.E. Tuttle Co., 1970

The Native Hawaiian Land Trust Task Force. *The Prophetic Vision of Ke'ōpūolani, The Sacred Queen of Hawai'i*. Hawai'i: Hawaiian Almanac Publishing, 1982

Oliver, D. *Ancient Tahitian Society 3 vols*. Honolulu: University Press of Hawaii, 1974

Orbell, M. *The Natural World of the Maori*. Dobbs Ferry, N.Y.: Sheridan House, 1985

Pei Te Hurinui. *King Potatau*. Wellington N.Z.: The Polynesian Society, 1959

Pettazzoni, R. *The All Knowing God; Researches into Early Religion and Culture*. London: Methuen, 1956

Piercy, L. *Hawaii Truth Stranger Than Fiction*. Honolulu: Fisher, 1985

—. *Hawai'i's Missionary Saga*. Honolulu: Mutual Publishing, 1992

Potter, N. & Kasdon, L. *Hawai'i Our Island State*. Ohio: Charles E. Merrill Books, 1964

Pratt, G. *Samoan Dictionary*. Samoa: London Missionary Society Press, 1862

Pukui, M. & Elbert, S. *Hawaiian-English Dictionary*. Honolulu: University of Hawai'i Press, 1957

Pukui, M., Haertig, E.W., Lee, C. *Nānā I Ke Kumu*. 2 vols. Honolulu: Hui Hanai, 1972

Richards, W. *Memoir of Ke'ōpūolani*. Boston: Crocker & Brewster, 1825

Rose, R. *Hawai'i: The Royal Isles*. Honolulu: Bishop Museum, 1980

Ryan, P.M. *The New Dictionary of Modern Maori*. Auckland, N.Z.: Heinemann, 1974

Schmitt, R. *Historical Statistics of Hawai'i*. Honolulu: University of Hawai'i Press, 1977

—. *The Missionary Censuses of Hawai'i*. Honolulu: Bishop Museum, 1973

Schmidt, W. *The Origin and Growth of Religion*. Trans. Rose, H. J. London: Methuen & Co., 1935

Shook, E. *Ho'oponopono*. Honolulu: The East-West Center, 1985

Shortland, E. *Traditions and Superstitions of the New Zealanders*. 1856; rpt. New York: AMS Press, 1980

Siers, J. *Tonga*. Wellington, N.Z.: Millwood Press, 1978

Sinclair, K. ed. *The Oxford Illustrated History of New Zealand*. Auckland, N.Z.: Oxford University Press

Silverman, J. *Ka'ahumanu, Molder of Change*. Honolulu: Friends of the Judiciary History Cntr. of Hawai'i, 1987

Smith, P. *Journal of the Polynesian Society*. supplement. vol. 29-30 Wellington, N.Z.: The Polynesian Society, 1920

Sterling, E. & Summers, C. Editors. *Sites of O'ahu*. Honolulu: Bishop Museum, 1978

Stimson, J.F. *The Cult of Kiho-tuma*. Bulletin 111. Bernice P. Bishop Museum. Honolulu: The Museum, 1933

Taylor, C. "Tales About Hawai'i." *Honolulu Star Bulletin*. Newspaper Honolulu: Monday, June 19, 1961

Taylor, E. A. "The Cult of 'Iolani." *Paradise of the Pacific*. Dec. 1931

Taylor, P. *Kapi'olani: A Memorial*. Honolulu: Grieve, 1897

Te Haupapa-o-tane. *'Io, The Supreme God, and Other Gods Of The Maori* vol. 29-30. *Journal of the Polynesian Society*. Wellington, N.Z.: The Polynesian Society, 1920

Tregear, E. *Maori-Polynesian Comparative Dictionary*. Wellington, N.Z.: Lyon & Blair, 1891

Thrum, T. *Hawaiian Folk Tales*. Chicago: A.C. McClurg & Co., 1912

Twain, M. *Roughing It*. Hartford: American Publishing Co., 1886

Valeri, V. trans. Wissing, P. *Kingship and Sacrifice, Ritual and Society in Ancient Hawaii*. Chicago: University of Chicago Press, 1985

Whatahoro, H.T. *The Lore of the Whare-Wananga*. pt. 1. vol. 3-4. *Memoirs of the Polynesian Society*. Trans. Smith, P. New Plymoth, N.Z.: Thomas Avery, 1913

White, J. *The Ancient History of the Maori, His Mythology and Traditions* vols. 1 & 2. Wellington: George Didsbury, Government Printer, 1887

Wisniewski, R. *The Rise and Fall of the Hawaiian Kingdom*. Honolulu: Pacific Basin Ent., 1979

Word Publishing. *The Everyday Bible, New Century Version*. Dallas, TX: Word Publishing, 1988

Wood. P. "The Way Forward." *Hana Hou!* Magazine. Vol. 9, No. 2 April/ May 2006

## *God of Light, God of Darkness*

For further information please contact the author at:

Aloha Ke Akua Ministries
P.O. Box 492325
Keaau, HI 96749

**Online orders:** www.alohakeakua.org

**Bulk, bookstore, school, club, ministry or church orders, inquire at:** sales@alohakeakua.org